Colonial Image of Malay Adat Laws

Social Sciences in Asia

Edited by
Vineeta Sinha
Syed Farid Alata
Chan Kwok Bun

VOLUME 6

Colonial Image of Malay Adat Laws

A Critical Appraisal of Studies on Adat Laws in the Malay Peninsula during the Colonial Era and Some Continuities

by
Noor Aisha Abdul Rahman

BRILL
LEIDEN • BOSTON
2006

This book is printed on acid-free paper.

Library of Congress Cataloging-in-Publication Data

Noor Aisha Abdul Rahman.
Colonial image of Malay Adat laws : a critical appraisal of studies on Adat laws in the Malay Peninsula during the colonial era and some continuities / by Noor Aisha Abdul Rahman.
p. cm. — (Social sciences in Asia, ISSN 1567-2794 ; v. 6)
Includes bibliographical references and index.
ISBN-13: 978-90-04-15056-0
ISBN-10: 90-04-15056-0 (pbk. : alk. paper)
1. Adat law—Malaysia—History. 2. Islamic law—Malaysia—History. I. Title. II. Series.

KPG449.3.N66 2006
340.5'2595—dc22

2006043878

ISSN 1567-2794
ISBN 90 04 15056 0

PRINTED IN THE NETHERLANDS

For my family

CONTENTS

INTRODUCTION

This book attempts primarily to analyze studies on adat laws in the Malay Peninsula by several prominent colonial administrators and scholars whose works are generally acknowledged as pioneering and authoritative expositions of the subject. It seeks to examine their contribution towards the understanding of Malay adat laws as well as to ascertain whether, if at all, their portrayal of the laws suffers misconceptions or inadequacies. Should there be any such shortcomings, this book hopes to identify these and show how they impair a balanced representation of the laws.

The term Malay adat laws is used herein to denote those aspects of Malay customs that have legal consequences. Essentially, it refers to those customs which, if breached, will be met by the application of force by persons whose authority is recognized and sanctioned by society.[1] In the field of adat law studies the usage of this term owes its origins to Dutch adat law scholars such as Snouck Hurgronje (1906). Snouck was perhaps the first to point out that since customary practices amongst most of the people in the Malay Archipelago were denominated by the Arabic word "adat", it would be fruitful to speak of adat that has legal consequences, "adat law."[2]

The colonial administrators and scholars whose works we are examining spearheaded the task of collating Malay legal codes, digests and proverbial sayings. They also translated, classified, enumerated, compared and contrasted adat law with English law. More significantly, they evaluated these laws in the light of their perceptions of progress and humanity. Their salient ideas and perspectives are so entrenched and pervasive that they continue to influence contemporary discourse on important aspects of law and Malay society. Though not a major thrust, this book touches upon some of these continuities.

---

[1] For works highlighting the distinction between customs with legal consequences and other social rules, please refer to, K.N. Llewellyn and E. Adamson Hoebel (1941) 20–29 and E. Adamson Hoebel (1954) 18–28.

[2] For a discussion on the origin of this term in adat law studies, please refer to Holleman (1981), 5, and Ter Haar (Hoebel 1984), 5.

In this study attention will be focused upon portraying and analyzing dominant representations of Malay adat laws that consistently recur in the scholarship of colonial scholars. It will also investigate how the writers approached the study of Malay laws. Attempts will be made to discover unstated assumptions, if any, the sources that influenced their opinions and how these affected a balanced, objective and accurate understanding of Malay adat laws. Significant implications arising from their perceptions of adat laws will also be analyzed.

Since we are dealing with the study of ideas about Malay laws, some insight into the sociology of knowledge may serve useful. Of relevance is the principle that ideas are rooted in particular social and historical milieu and that perspectives differ depending on the interests and social groups they represent (Mannheim, 1936: 266–279).[3] Hence the study of ideas on Malay adat laws cannot be isolated from the social and historical contexts from which they emerged and evolved. This book will therefore take into consideration the contextual conditions that influenced the writers' selection and conceptualization of adat laws.

Historically, writings on Malay adat laws in the Peninsula began with the expansion of colonialism since the early 19th century. They formed part of the wider, consistent and systematic attempts by colonial authorities generally at constructing and portraying the culture, history, tradition and civilization of the people over whom they governed or controlled politically. Lodged within the interplay of knowledge and power, such efforts contributed to the development of a discipline referred to by Said as Orientalism (1978). In its academic sense, Orientalism is characterized by the rise of specialization involving the study of various Oriental cultures and traditions that had succumbed to colonial rule (Macfie, 2000: 346). It is manifested in scholarly attempts at classifying and investigating types of knowledge deemed essential to the colonial government within the conquered territories. Within the classification of knowledge, native law has received tremendous significance and occupied a central place.[4]

[3] See also his discussion on "style of thought" in "Conservative Thought" in Essays on Sociology and Social Psychology (1953).

[4] For a discussion on the attempts to create and enumerate modalities of knowledge of the subjugated territories arising out of the rise and entrenchment of imperial power, see the introduction by (Cohn, 1996).

As a style of thought, Orientalism is based upon a fundamental distinction between the west and the Orient in which the superiority of the West and the latter's inferiority are unquestioned. This epistemological divide is inextricably tied to political domination and authority over the Orient creating a network of interests which inevitably penetrates perspectives and representations on any subject involving the Orient such that what emerges is a certain consistency of ideas. Arising from the position of relative superiority, such studies are distinguished by the Oriental's historical absence in the discourse in which he is the object of study (Said, 1978: 2–8). This mode of thought reveals characteristic limitations that include ethnocentrism, overgeneralizations, stereotyping, bias and prejudice. The Orient is often dogmatically perceived as an unchanging abstraction. Such scholarship also reflects the tendency to succumb to analysis divorced from significant contributions from the social sciences. Equally pertinent is the partial selection of issues and problems that distorts understanding. That these traits have adverse effects on Malay studies generally has not escaped attention (Alwee, 2002). This book will examine to what extent this style of thought operates in representations of Malay adat laws in colonial scholarship and its ramifications.

In our attempts to understand colonial preoccupation with Malay adat laws and "unmask" the factors that influence their ideas, the concept of ideology as defined by Karl Mannheim is utilized (Mannheim, 1936: 40) Ideology in the sense used by Mannheim, reflects the thinking of ruling groups in society. These groups have become so intensively interest-bound to a situation that they are no longer able to see certain facts that would undermine their sense of domination. The collective unconscious of the group obscures the real condition of society both to itself and to others. In scholarship, the influence of ideology is manifested not only in the formation of concepts but also in the selection, perception and analysis of problems. The usage of ideology as a conceptual tool to understand and evaluate colonial scholarship on the Malays has been pioneered by Syed Hussein Alatas in his work *The Myth of the Lazy Native* (1977). Utilizing the sociology of knowledge approach, Alatas argues that the dominant image of the indolent native that originated in the 16th century is a function of the ideology of colonial capitalism that seeks to justify European intervention and its alleged aim of modernizing and civilizing Malay society. Alatas' perspective is highly relevant to our attempt at analyzing colonial scholarship on Malay laws and legal institutions since they form an integral aspect of the wider colonial discourse on Malay culture and society. Utilizing the concept of ideology, this study hopes to reveal the motives that justify the focus on native laws and the extent to which it shapes and conditions the views, opinions and judgments expressed by the authors.

This book is motivated by several considerations. Generally, efforts at comprehending the institutions of the Malays have long been in progress. Law, being an integral aspect of society and culture, our appraisal of studies on Malay adat laws is perceived as part of such attempts at understanding Malay culture. In view of this, should any misleading notions or misrepresentations of adat law be discovered, it is hoped that alternative explanations can be provided which will enhance our understanding. It is generally believed that the laws of any society mirror its ethos and embody its essential ideals and ethical principles. As the renowned jurist Oliver Wendell Holmes aptly remarked (Holmes, 1920: 170): "The law is the witness and external deposit of our moral life. Its history is the history of the moral development of the race." A study of ideas about Malay laws is pertinent since they can contribute to our understanding of those ideas and values of the Malays that are strong enough to attain the expression of law. This study can also be justified by the fact that, although there have been many works on the subject, none to the best of my knowledge, completely shares the aims and focus of the present work.

Numerous writings exist on the subject of adat laws in the Malay Peninsula. The amount of literature on this area well exceeds a hundred titles. However, this book is not intended to be an exhaustive appraisal of these materials. Attention will be focused only on several major works on the subject. These are the writings of Stamford Raffles (1835), Richard Winstedt (1953, 1956), E.N. Taylor (1937, 1948), W.E. Maxwell (1884), Frank Swettenham (1955), and John Crawford (1820). They provide the conceptual boundaries and are generally regarded as authoritative expositions of adat laws. Indeed, it is difficult to find works on Malay laws that do not make mention of their views and perceptions. The present work also attempts to reveal some continuity in their ideas and perspectives on more recent scholarship pertaining to Malay laws. In this regard, some aspects of the works of Josselin de Jong (1960), M.B. Hooker (1968) and Michael Peletz (1988) will be examined. Their scholarship on various aspects of adat is perhaps among the more prominent on the subject and, as such, their views and ideas deserve consideration. It is important to state that in critically evaluating selected aspects of their works, we do not disregard or underestimate their contributions that are of value.

Various sources that portray the Malay adat laws have been utilized in this study. They include the Malay legal digests and several old Malay texts. The former include the *Melaka Legal Code* (*Undang-Undang Melaka*), the *Kedah Legal Code* (*Undang-Undang Kedah*), the *Minangkabau Digest* from Perak, and the *Sungei Ujong Legal Code* (*Undang-Undang Sungei Ujong*). Some of the old Malay texts used are *The Malay Annals* (*Sejarah Melayu*), *Hikayat Raja-raja Pasai*, Bustan al-Salatin, Tuhfat-al-Nafis, and the works of Munshi Abdullah (1965). In addition, jurisprudential works and other sources on the Malays, relevant to an understanding of adat laws, are also of immense use to our study.

This book will be based on selected main themes. It begins with an exposition of the essential conception of the authors on adat laws. These constitute the materials for subsequent analysis. Since we are dealing with their ideas on the subject, it is only appropriate that a portrayal of their studies be presented along thematic rather than chronological lines. In Chapter Two, we attempt to assess the writers' understanding of the nature and attribute of Malay adat laws and examine their impact on the image of the laws.

Chapter Three focuses on a more specific theme pertaining to their perceptions of one of the major sources of Malay adat laws, namely Islam. It seeks to appraise their fundamental perceptions of the nature of this relationship and its ramifications. Adat land and inheritance laws are recurring themes in the studies. They will be reviewed in Chapter Four, which highlights and assesses the dominant issues in the studies of these aspects of adat while examining some of the implications that arise from their perceptions.

Yet another theme that has received considerable attention in the colonial studies and which is the focus of the final chapter is the issue of the legal rights and privileges of the Malay ruling class under adat laws. Our aim is to evaluate common perceptions among colonial writers on this aspect in the light of relevant Malay historical sources.

Finally, this book also seeks to demonstrate the impact of these studies in framing and defining the conceptual boundaries and understanding of Malay adat laws in contemporary scholarship. It is hoped that unravelling the problems pertaining to this field of study will contribute to a better understanding not only of the legal tradition of Malay society but also of Malay culture in general.

CHAPTER ONE

COLONIAL PERCEPTIONS OF MALAY ADAT LAWS

One of the pioneers in the study of Malay adat laws is the prominent British colonial administrator John Crawford. In his book *The History of the Indian Archipelago*, the author revealed his perceptions of the "spirit and character" of these laws (1967, 3: 75–6). Although Crawford's overall concern lay in portraying the laws of native societies of South East Asia, our interest in his writing is confined to his specific evaluation of Malay adat laws. However, general remarks and observations on the condition of native laws as a whole, by which the author intended to include Malay laws, will also be examined.

Crawford's conceptions are not confined to specific legal questions. Rather, it is pertinent to note that he attempted to deal with the entire system of these laws. Based on the written codes of law found in these societies, Crawford examined the history and arrangement of these laws, the forms of its judiciary, and its "civil" and "penal" laws.

It can be said that Crawford subscribed to the view that Malay laws are primitive, backward and inadequate in dealing with important aspects of social life. In general, his description of the adat does not contain anything positive. Instead, he highlighted to a large extent that the adat is averse to certain fundamental humanitarian principles.

A clear instance of Crawford's conception that Malay laws are primitive and backward is evident in his opinion on the arrangement of the laws. According to the author (1967, 3: 78), "[a]ll of them display a remarkable character of rudeness and barbarism. Institutions so imperfect, indeed, have never in all probability been, among any other people, committed to writing. No attempt is made in them at arrangement or classifications but the most incompatible matters are blended together and the forms of judicature, civil and criminal jurisprudence, maxims of morality and commercial regulations, are incongruously intermixed."

Primitive elements and the lack of refinement, according to Crawford, pervade even the substance of the law. In support of his view,

Crawford cited laws expressing the functions and conduct of judges, such as those exhorting impartiality, fair play and scrupulous conduct in the dispensation of justice. Though such laws are illustrated from the Javanese code, the author's argument extends to other native laws including the laws of the Melaka Legal Code which also contain more or less similar provisions. In his view, these laws are but "self-evident maxims" and "crude instructions" which (page 85) "could only thus pompously, be paraded in a very rude and early stage of social union, and of the science of ethics."

An extension of Crawford's attempts at showing that the laws are backward and lack refinement is further seen in his evaluation of what he calls "the civil laws of the society". He remarked that those laws governing sale and purchase are "sufficiently simple" due to the poverty of the masses and the usurpation of the soil by the sovereign. Furthermore (page 96), he added that "loans, as in other rude states of society, where neither law nor morals encourage integrity in commercial transactions, are usually made on pledges." The same perception extends to his assessment of the law of letting and hiring, which he describes (page 94) as "scanty and ill-defined." Crawford also pointed out what he considers as "universal custom" in the native laws which allows for debt bondage (page 98). Even the law on evidence is subjected to the same evaluative judgment, as is evident in Crawford's remark (page 87) that "the rules of evidence, as among all barbarous people are arbitrary and capricious."

The penal laws of the natives are also subjected to evaluation. Not only are they portrayed as extremely harsh and severe, in some instances they are shown to be averse to fundamental humanitarian values. For instance, according to the author (page 104), "punishments are characterized by arbitrary violence, rather than by refinement in cruelty." When compared to the laws of the Hindus and the Chinese, native laws, according to Crawford (pages 104–5) "show a much less regard for human life. Death is the punishment of a hundred trifling offences and is awarded with a wantonness that shocks the humanity of civilisation."

Crawford also vividly described the varieties of capital punishment which, he believed, differed from those of more civilized nations: "The modes in which execution is effected illustrate the character of the people. Strangulation, by suspending the body from the neck, as among us, or decapitation, as so frequent with the greater nations of Asia, are never practiced.... The most familiar mode of violent death among them is stabbing with the kris, and this they transfer to their legal executions." He further added that this form of punishment is uncivilized from the European point of view because, "Stabbing with a kris is an uncertain mode of inflicting death, and conveys, at least to the European mind, the impression of savage ferocity." (pages 108–9). Furthermore (page 112), he also cited as one of the "most remarkable and instructive characteristics of the laws", differences in their allotment of punishment based on the rank of the offender.

Equally pertinent is Crawford's assertion that the law cannot adequately ensure the protection of life and property of the society concerned. Hence, according to the author, theft and robbery frequently occur (page 114). In his view, "the imperfect state of law and government" (page 120) also results in a large share of the right of avenging wrongs being left in the hands of private persons. According to Crawford (page 120), "the law even expressly interdicts all interference when there appears a character of fairness in the quarrels." Crawford also expressed his disgust for laws allowing the power of revenge to be delegated to individuals hired for the occasion with the permission of judicial authority (page 120–22). His perception of the inhumane values underlying the law is best reflected in his assertion that "[i]t is remarkable that there is not, in any language of the Indian islands, words equivalent to ours to murder, or murderer; no term which express[es] the horror which we attach to these. In these tongues, to murder is simply (page 124) "to kill" and a murderer is no more than "one [who] kills". Human life can be of little value among a people whose language is incapable of making this great moral distinction."

Yet another prominent colonial writer and administrator who pioneered efforts and showed keen interest in the study of Malay laws was Stamford Raffles. Like Crawford, Raffles perceived these laws to be backward and primitive. Such an evaluative judgment can be clearly discerned in the following passage, in which Raffles urged for the need to collate these laws. According to Raffles (1835, 30–1): "From the comparative rude and uncivilized character of the Malay nation, learned disquisition is not to be looked for but simple ideas, simply expressed, may illustrate character better than scientific or refined composition. And in this point of view, however local or particular the subject may be, the institutions and regulations of so extensive a maritime nation must be interesting."

Raffles also perceived the law as the primary factor impeding progress and the general well being of the Malays. Such a conception is clearly revealed in Raffles' attempts at diagnosing the problem of degeneration of the Malays. According to Raffles (page 98), "[n]othing has tended more decidedly to the deterioration of the Malay character than the want of a well defined and generally acknowledged system of the law."

The author further attempted to determine the factors that led to the decline of the Malays. He strongly perceived that it was the influence of Islam that had a negative impact upon the traditional laws of the Malays. Raffles showed a high regard for the ancient laws of the Malays that existed prior to the coming of Islam. He believed that the failure of Islam to synthesize with the original laws of the Malays brought about diversification in the realm of law which in turn opened the gates to oppression and capricious rule. Raffles explained the problem as follows:

> The Malay nations had in general made considerable progress in civilization before the introduction of the religion of Islam among them. They had, accordingly, regular institutions of their own, some of which were probably of considerable antiquity such as those of the Javanese, Bugis and Macassar tribes. As these appear to have been generally derived from the Indian nations and were radically different from those of the Arabs, some difficulty appears to have occurred, in adapting them to the general tenor of Mohamedan law, and diverse anomalous institutions appear accordingly to have sprung up in different states. These occur in every department of public law, whether commercial, civil or criminal and are recited in the Undang-Undang and Adat Melayu which are the systems of national law among the Malays.... Hence there is in almost every state a constant struggle between the adherents of the old Malay usages and the Hajis and other religious persons who are desirous of introducing the laws of the Arabs, in order to increase their own consequence. The evils which result from this complex and ill-defined system are both numerous and important, as they respect the most essential interests of society, and afford an opening for caprice and tyranny of their rulers and general insecurity both of person and property (pages 98–9).

Raffles also portrayed what he perceived as inadequacies in the law in regulating fundamental aspects of human life. Retribution and retaliation were left in the hands of private individuals without recourse to a proper system of established arbitration. Such conceptions of the state of Malay laws are clearly revealed in Raffles' attempts at explaining the significance of the feud in Malay society as compared with the European nation. According to Raffles,

> The creeses is to the Malay what the practice of duelling is to European nations. There are certain points in the composition of every man's notion which cannot be regulated by courts of law; the property, the life, the character of the European is protected by law, but yet there are some points and these are the very points on which all society hinges, which are not protected. In support of these, he condemns the law which stigmatizes him as a murderer and the very men who made the laws still say he is right. Neither the property, the life nor the character of the Malay is secured by law—he proudly defends them with his own hand whenever they are endangered. The readiness with which an injury is thus redressed has a wonderful effect in the prevention of injuries; and except in warlike enterprise, the Malay is seldom known to draw his criss, unless in defense of what he considers his honour (page 288).

Of all branches of Malay laws, maritime and commercial regulations were the ones with which Raffles was predominantly concerned. Generally, he perceived Malay maritime laws as degrading and uncivilised. Such an evaluation is evident in his following assessment with respect to the powers of the sea captains. In his words (page 41),

> the power of life and death, vested in the Nakhoda, or captain of a vessel, may be considered as purely Malay, or at any rate to have had its origin in the Eastern islands: the Arabs from whom alone they could have borrowed a foreign seacode, not possessing . . . any treaties whatever on maritime law, or in any instance admitting the authority of the Nakhoda to inflict capital punishments. In this point of view, the paper . . . may tend . . . to account for some of the numerous peculiarities of a nation generally believed to act on most occasions solely from individual will and ferocious passion.

Such propositions, opinions and judgments on Malay adat laws persisted, even after a century or so, in the writings of subsequent colonial administrators such as Wilkinson and Winstedt. Though their writings reflected the perspectives and themes of the earlier writers, they also refined and extended the earlier arguments and observations. Like their predecessor Raffles, they viewed the influence of Islam on adat laws as destructive and negative. This is evident from the contrasting evaluative judgments of the authors on the Adat Perpateh and the Adat Temenggong. For purposes of clarity, it is necessary to explain what the writers mean by these two terms, as used in their works.

Despite some variations, the writers generally share a broad definition of these terms.[1] By Adat Perpateh, they mean the laws and customs of the matrilineal Minangkabau population of Negri Sembilan, whose ancestors had migrated from Sumatra. On the other hand, they use the term Adat Temenggong to designate the customary laws of the other Malay states which were organized along patrilineal lines. They also perceived that, unlike the Adat Perpateh, the Adat Temenggong is largely influenced by Hinduism and Islam.

In fact, their rigid evaluative division between these two legal systems was borne out of what they believed was the influence of Islam and, to some extent, Hinduism, on the Adat Temenggong. Consequently, the Adat Perpateh, which they conceived as being the original laws of the Malays prior to the coming of Islam and Hinduism, was conferred with positive values and held in high esteem. On the other hand, the Adat Temenggong, perceived as the product of Hinduistic and Islamic influences, was subjected to severe criticisms. Thus, in the words of Wilkinson (Hooker, 1970: 31–2):

> If therefore Malay law is studied in the light of Malay history, we can easily understand why the adat Temenggong . . . should cover so many important states and yet compare so unfavourably with the adat Perpateh of the humble villages of Negri Sembilan. We have no reason to suppose that the adat Temenggong ever was a consistent and coherent system. It simply represents the old Minangkabau jurisprudence, the true law of the Malays, in a state of disintegration after many centuries of exposure to the influence of Hindu despotism and Moslem law.

In the same vein, Winstedt remarked (1953: 98):

> Put its customary provisions alongside the despotic rule and brutal hybrid law of the patriarchal Malay states and at once it is apparent why this matriarchal law commands the passionate regard of the Minangkabaus as a Magna Carta or as they express it, 'a couch for the sleeper, a shelter for the wayfarer, a ship for the navigator, a heritage for the farmer.' No Raja ever dared to tamper with its validity and no Muslim Kathi to challenge its orthodox principle. It was safe in the keeping of a democracy of inland agriculturalists impervious to foreign influence.

[1] Winstedt for instance, unlike the other writers defines the adat Perpateh as "Law of Ministers" and adat Temeggong as "Law of the Minister for War and Police" (Winstedt, 1956: 91).

Negative evaluations of Malay adat laws, as conceived by Crawford and Raffles, recurred and were developed consistently in the evaluation of the adat Temenggong by Wilkinson and Winstedt. Backward, oppressive, brutal, inhumane, despotic and unjust; these were some of the value-loaded adjectives used to describe this system of Malay laws. Wilkinson for instance (Hooker, 1970: 10), denounced the entire Adat Temenggong as one which "brutalised the people." Furthermore (page 7), he evaluated the adat as "autocratic". It was also perceived as a system which served the vested interest of the ruling class. Thus the adat, he remarked (page 7), is "supported by Malay princes and finds expression in long legal digests drawn up by court scribes for the glorification of the Raja and for the purpose of displaying their own learning." Moreover, the laws were also viewed as institutionalizing an oppressive feudal hierarchy. Far from being socially beneficial, they were considered petty and trivial (page 35).

Not only is the law perceived as interest bound, it was also judged as arbitrary and exploitative in its system of administering justice. The following remarks by Wilkinson (page 9) illustrate the point:

> The interests of a Malay chief lay in the direction of exacting heavy fines, reducing offenders to slavery under him, and vindicating his authority by the cruel punishment of any man who dared to gainsay him or disregard his commands. The justice of a Malay prince, even when impartial, was a cruel and pitiless justice, seeking to deter rather than to reform.

In fact, Wilkinson conceived (page 34) despotic administrative authority as one of the constituent elements of the law, which was also judged as inadequate in providing continued peace and protection of life, as illustrated in the following assertion:

> Every commoner, for his own protection, had to buy the patronage of a powerful chief. If he was wronged, he asked the chief to take up his case; if the chief dared not do anything, the injured party had either to abandon the suit or to take the law into his own hands. Vendettas were frequent and bitter. The judges sat armed and did not hesitate to kill the prisoner if he insulted them or questioned their jurisdiction or impartiality as he might very well do (page 37).

Such evaluative assertions were also found in Winstedt's writing. Like Raffles, Winstedt subscribed to the view that diversification in sources of law opened the way for capricious rule. His following remarks (1956: 100) reveal this point:

> Both the Malacca and Pahang digests . . . are marked by contemporary inconsistencies that left scope for an autocratic ruler to follow customary, Hindu or Muslim law as he pleased. In medieval Malacca, therefore, no one can ever have been certain of the provisions of the patriarchal police law, designed with its public cages of starved and mutilated criminals to cow a cosmopolitan port mob.

Like Wilkinson, Winstedt also perceived the Adat Temenggong to be barbaric and cruel. Instances cited (page 101) include the right of a victim of a blow to kill within three days a man who had struck him. To reinforce his view that the Adat Temenggong showed a disregard for human life, Winstedt noted (page 101) that in the Pahang digest, "anyone except a lunatic may be killed for knocking at a door by night". Furthermore, the forms of sanctions the law prescribed were portrayed as brutal. These included impalement, mutilation, amputation and many other severe forms of punishment.

Again, like Wilkinson, Winstedt also viewed the administrators of the law as biased and arbitrary. Thus, according to him (page 103),

> at an autocratic court, even a dream might be accounted as good evidence . . . When evidence was as clear as a "white fowl flying by day", there was still the danger that an aristocratic judge, misled by the casuistry of Muslim pundits displayed to impress Malay royalty, might come to a decision so ingenious as to be at once absurd and iniquitous.

In stark contrast to the negative evaluation of the Adat Temenggong, the authors expressed a deep sense of admiration for the Adat Perpateh. The Adat Perpateh was portrayed as the living law of the Malays, embodying sound and constructive values that were socially beneficial. Thus, according to Wilkinson (Hooker, 1970: pages 7–8), the adat Perpateh is "democratic", it "addresses itself to the commons", it is "based upon actual experience", it is "known to all" and has the "full force of public opinion behind it, reference to it is sufficient to compel even an unjust judge to do justice to the litigants before him." Furthermore, Wilkinson also conceived (page 9) the law as "lenient" and "humane" such that "death, enslavement and exile were extreme penalties that could only be applied to incorrigible offenders." "We therefore find," according to the author, "that the Adat Perpateh was an extremely mild system of law, lenient to first offenders and always ready to condone a wrong if due restitution was made."

Simplicity was yet another perceived merit of this adat. As Wilkinson remarked (page 19):

> The simplicity of the law of Minangkabau was its strength. If a suitor had a perfectly clear case, he either got what he wanted or made it clear to the whole countryside that he was being unjustly kept out of his rights. He could not put off with any misrepresentation of a law that the very children of the country knew and understood.

According to Wilkinson (page 30), so revered is this system of law by the Malays that it "was never to be amended or altered".

It is obvious that English law served as the ultimate frame of reference which conditioned the author's evaluative judgments of the Adat Perpateh and the Adat Temenggong. This is clearly revealed in Wilkinson's assertion (page 10) that "when compared with English law, the Adat Temenggong seems very faulty indeed; it is crude and primitive in its legal theories, uncertain and unmethodical in its pronouncements, cruel and brutalising in its punishment." Even the "primitive" Adat Perpateh which he revered (page 10) "bears comparison with English law best."

The writers also sought to portray the positive influence of English law. Winstedt (1956: 108), for instance asserted that "it was English jurisprudence that first showed the Malay any distinction between constitutional, criminal and civil law". Furthermore, he strongly suggested (page 94) that English law was more impartial and just. Such an evaluation was also evident in Wilkinson's appraisal. The author was of the opinion that English rule brought about immense improvement to the well being of the Malays, in particular the Malay masses (Hooker, 1970: 35).

Another consistent theme was the relationship between Islam and Malay adat laws. Wilkinson (page 7), for example, asserted that Islam and the adat laws were "absolutely irreconcilable" and "conflicting". According to him, "the Malays as good Moslems, profess to accept the legal teachings of Islam even where those teachings conflict with the local adat; they pretend indeed to regard the adat as explanatory of Muslim law or as supplementary to it. All this is mere fiction; the three legal systems are absolutely irreconcilable."

Wilkinson also perceived that, in actuality, the influence of Islam on adat law is superficial and nominal. Thus he remarked (page 20), "In theory, the Minangkabau Malays are good Muhammadans and are bound to accept the whole of the Muhammadan law, but in practice, they limit that acceptance to matters in which it does not disagree with their own customs. When it comes to choosing between the adat and hukum shara', they allow the latter to go to the wall."

Furthermore, he conceived Islamic law as static and arbitrary. According to him (1908: 67), the law is "theoretically unchangeable." Moreover, he also subscribed to the view (page 46) that the *hadith* are but "a confused mass of rulings" and that its validity was "decided by dream and prayers rather than by the weight of serious evidence."

The problem of the relationship between Islam and adat law has also been substantially discussed in the work of M.B. Hooker, a post-independence scholar on adat laws. Before proceeding to portray the author's views on the nature of their relationship, it is necessary to state Hooker's conception of Islamic law.

Like Wilkinson, Hooker (1984: 30) subscribed to the view that Islamic law is theoretically unchangeable. Its doctrinal principles fossilised as early as the tenth century. As such, the efforts of subsequent jurists were confined merely to textual commentaries and elaboration of the established doctrinal principles, while the judges' task was merely to apply these already formulated doctrines to cases in dispute. Hooker believed that the *sharia* law does not develop in relation to the problems of society. Such a conception is implied in his assertion that (page 30), "the *sharia* is, pre-eminently, a law of the book, a jurist's law, and this of course always implies a certain degree of artificiality."

Another indication of Hooker's conception that Islamic law is stagnant is revealed in his understanding of the *ijma* as a source of Islamic law. According to Hooker (page 31),

> *Ijma*, the agreement of qualified legal scholars of a given generation, was the concept developed to describe the result of scholastic endeavour. Once such a result was known in a particular case, further development was not possible: 'the door of *ijtihad* was closed'. From the tenth century onwards all that was possible was an imitation (*taqlid*) of established doctrine, which meant detailed commentary and the production of authoritative legal texts for each school of jurisprudence.

Hooker's conception of the *sharia* as a revealed system of law that is absolute and stagnant leads him to assert (page 3) that it "may not fit easily into or combine with non-revelationary realities, whether economic, social, political, ecological, or legal." More specifically, he subscribed to the view that the *sharia* which arose and developed out of a particular social and historical milieu is alien to the culture of the Malays. The consequence of its imposition in native states leads to a relationship of tension between it and the local adat (page 3). In fact, Hooker conceives the legal history of Islam in Southeast Asia as a history of tension between an absolute scheme of (revealed) obligation and its adaptation to local cultural realities (page 36).

According to Hooker, this characteristic relationship between adat law and Islam is manifested in the legal digests as inconsistencies as to the sources of law, sovereignty of law, reality of law and the definition of obligation. Hooker reveals (page 36) that, in all these aspects, there is a persistence of non-Islamic elements existing together with the Islamic ones. "The adat," he claims, "cannot be wished away."

Like Wilkinson, Hooker perceives the relationship between Islam and the adat Perpateh as irreconcilable and contradictory in many essential aspects. Provisions found in the Malay legal digests that seek to explain the complementary relationship between Islam and adat as sources of law, are viewed by Hooker (page 19) as "a conscious attempt to resolve obvious differences."

The conception of the nature of the relationship between adat and Islam and the extent and degree of influence of the latter on the former as revealed in some of the writings above also condition the perceptions on specific rules of adat laws such as those pertaining to inheritance. One of the main exponents of adat law on inheritance is E.N. Taylor, a prominent member of the colonial legal service.

Taylor conceptualized the problem of inheritance in the framework of perceived conflict between adat and Islamic law. Like his predecessors, he viewed the two legal systems as irreconcilable (Hooker, 1970: 162–63). Taylor argued that adat principles governing inheritance accorded with practical wisdom and were more suitable to the condition of the Malays. Essentially, the reason he provided was that Islamic law, having originated from a different social context, thus could not practically serve the needs of the Malays (1937: 4–5).

In his writing and in his judgments on cases in dispute, Taylor expressed a preference for the adat. For instance, he strongly believed that the adat law on distribution of property is more just when compared to Islamic law (page 10), for "in the vast majority of Malay families, 1/8 would not provide the widow with subsistence." Furthermore, Taylor also expressed the view that the Islamic law of inheritance brings about destructive consequences in the long run. Its rules governing the division of land and adjustments in terms of money, where portions cannot be so arranged have, according to Taylor (Hooker, 1970: 238), led to serious impoverishment of the peasantry.

In spite of Malay demands for the application of the *shariah* in the distribution of acquired property (harta carian), Taylor was adamant (pages 189–91) in insisting that Malays generally desired the continued application of their traditional inheritance laws. He also subscribed (page 191) to the view that the introduction of the *fara'id* would only result in the collapse of the social structure in the adat Perpateh areas.[2] Malay attempts at reconciling the adat with Islamic law on inheritance were perceived by Taylor as being the product of muddled thinking (1937: 55).

Taylor's supposition that adat inheritance law conflicted with Islamic law and principles is manifested in many relatively recent works by prominent scholars whose writings touched upon the influence of and relationship between adat and Islam on Malay social and legal institutions. Amongst these, the writings of Josselin de Jong (1960) and Michael Peletz (1988) will be highlighted as illustrations.

De Jong's analysis of adat-Islam crisis in Rembau, Negri Sembilan in 1951 over the issue of inheritance law among contesting groups of Malay leaders and their followers deserves consideration, for it has been generally accepted by many scholars as an accurate depiction of the relationship between adat and Islam during much of the twentieth century.[3] Generally, the author perceived a radical difference between the two systems, affecting one's person and property. Peletz, whose anthropological studies on Negri Sembilan are generally well known, likewise subscribed to a similar opinion, although he noted that there were many areas, particularly in relation to moral values, where the adat and Islam harmonized. In this context, he asserted that this "should not deter us from realizing that Malays throughout Negri Sembilan have long been aware of certain areas wherein adat and Islam prescribe divergent, even conflicting action" even if "conscious knowledge of these areas of divergence was probably quite limited in distribution over a century ago." Peletz's perception that the adat and Islamic law on inheritance conflicted is revealed in his assertion that (1981: 19–20):

---

[2] Fara'id is the technical term for the fixed shares in an estate (1/2, 1/4, 1/3, 1/8, 2/3, and 1/16) which are given to heirs on the basis of the Quran (IV 11–2 and 176). These Quranic verses aim at modifying a system of purely agnatic succession under which only men can inherit, in favour of the nearest female relatives (including half brothers on the mother's side), the spouse and also the father (who is protected against being excluded by existing male descendents) See Th.W. Juynboll, 1965, 783.

[3] See for instance the view of MG Peletz, 1988: p 123.

> it is imperative to note that Islamic doctrines, to take one example, sanction certain marriages and post marital residence patterns which are strongly discouraged by adat . . . Islamic texts, moreover, do not differentiate, as does adat, between *harta pesaka* and *harta sepencarian* (that is between clan controlled "ancestral" property, on the one hand, and that which is "acquired" either jointly by spouses during the course of their marriage or by unmarried persons, on the other). Consequently Islam permits inheritance practices and other aspects of property transfer forbidden by adat. In addition, Islamic sources do not recognize the concept of corporate land ownership, a concept of crucial importance in the agriculturally based adat system. As a result, Islamic law not only disavows claims to property if they are based solely on membership in corporate kin groups but also regards certain adat traditions associated with property transfer as contrary to and forbidden by the Koran. Furthermore, the legal conventions of Islam specify that a male child is entitled to receive inheritance shares in the proportion of two to every one share allotted his sister. Adat, in contradistinction, while suggesting that all children regardless of sex deserve roughly equal portions of their parents' wealth, contains numerous provisions having the effect of prohibiting males from inheriting any property in the form of land.

Apart from the question of inheritance, writings on Malay adat laws also reveal concerted attempts at portraying the concept of Malay land tenure. Such studies are useful and pertinent to our appraisal in two important respects. Apart from revealing the factors which condition the writers' selection of problems and issues on Malay adat laws, these writings also constitute an essential part of adat law studies. As such, failure to take into account these works would render our evaluation incomplete.

Meticulous and diligent attempts at understanding adat land tenure are best manifested in the writings of the two prominent colonial administrators of their time, W.E. Maxwell and F.A. Swettenham. The issue of land tenure was of immense importance, not only to British administrators but also to the colonial capitalists. In the Malay Peninsula, land was perhaps one of the most significant factors by which the colonial power derived large revenues. It was also an important asset to British colonial planters and miners. As Maxwell himself explained (1964: 77):

> Besides persons in the service of the Native Governments who are brought, by their duties, into connection with native landholders, there is an independent class of British settlers—planters, miners and others—to whom it may be important to know what rights in contiguous land their native neighbours may have and how they are at liberty to alienate them.

Essentially, both Maxwell and Swettenham believed that the Malay sovereign had an absolute right to the soil. Thus, according to Swettenham (Maxwell, 1984: xiv), Malay land belonged to the *kerajaan.* Maxwell further offered an explanation for the origin of this doctrine. He perceived that it stemmed from the unquestioned right of the Malay sovereign to demand a proportion of the produce on land and to dispose of waste land. These privileges exercised by the Raja gradually led to the notion that the sovereign owned the land (1964: 91).

In some ways, the writers differed in their understanding of the rights of the Malay subjects to land. Maxwell, for instance, believed that, subject to the mandatory obligations which they must perform in the sovereign's interest, the Malay was the independent owner of a piece of land he had won for himself (page 92). Such an interest in land, however, Maxwell distinguished from the English conception of freehold or fee simple (page 122). He attempted to define this right as nothing more than a usufruct (page 91).

Swettenham, on the other hand, was of the opinion that the Malay peasant was not the owner of the land he occupied. He was merely a tenant-at-will and his occupation of the land depended purely upon the whim of the Malay ruler. Swettenham also maintained that because Malay subjects did not own the land on which they remained, they could not dispose of it at will (Maxwell, 1984: xiv). While Maxwell expressed keen support for the continued application of the Malay land tenure (1964: 154), Swettenham, by contrast, firmly sanctioned its abolition. His proposed substitute was the introduction of land law based upon English concepts of land tenure (Maxwell, 1984: xiv).

The previous discussion in this chapter has highlighted the salient concerns, views and ideas of several prominent colonial scholars/administrators and some continuities on the issue of Malay adat laws. We now move our attention, in the following chapter, to the examination of some major problems pertaining to these perceptions.

CHAPTER TWO

PROBLEMS CONCERNING THE CONCEPTUALIZATION OF MALAY ADAT LAWS

This chapter attempts to examine critically some significant problems in the conceptualization of Malay adat laws as found in the writings of Raffles, Crawford, Wilkinson and Winstedt. Many shortcomings are contained in these writings, which reveal especially some serious problems with regard to the conceptualization of Malay adat laws in relation to the society in which they operate. Some of the claims against the adat also fail to withstand the test of evidence provided by the substantive content of the laws. In addition, their views are marred by misrepresentations, logical fallacies, a lack of objectivity in appreciating the individuality of Malay laws due to a dominant conception of the superiority of English legal thought, as well as ideologically motivated attempts at denigrating the image of these laws. Furthermore, misleading and superficial judgments and opinions against the adat arise due to a failure to grasp the nature of the law and to take into consideration relevant historical data. In some respects, the style of thought in their discourse reveals the salient traits of Orientalism as characterised earlier.

An instance of such a misleading evaluation of Malay adat laws is evident in Raffles' diagnosis of the decline and degeneration of Malay society. As we saw in the previous chapter, Raffles singled out (1835: 98) Malay laws as the predominant cause of the problem, arguing that it was the want of a generally established and recognized system of laws regulating the most essential aspects of Malay social life that was the major responsible factor. In his opinion, it was largely the influence of Islam which, having failed to synthesize with indigenous laws brought about a "complex and ill-defined system of laws." This in turn opened the way for capricious rule and a general insecurity of person and property (pages 98–99).

Raffles was silent on the question of centuries of exploitation brought about by European domination, which had adverse repercussions and negative effects on the Malays, contributing to their eventual degeneration. Braddell's observations of the impact of the policies of European traders in the Malay Archipelago serve as a useful source of support. In illustrating the policies pursued in particular by the Dutch and the English, Braddell (1858: 322) succinctly remarked that

> the system . . . apparently a refinement of a more direct robbery on their predecessors, had in the end a prejudicial effect on the well being of the native states. Each party aimed at the possession of an exclusive right to trade . . . towards the natives a system was pursued such as being acknowledged, hitherto, among civilized nations. Whenever a trade had been collected at any port, by reason of its favourable position for commerce or the advantageous state of government, the Europeans settled themselves. Under the pretence of protecting their lives and property, they erected forts whose guns were turned upon the neighbouring town. They forced from the sovereigns of these ports, engagements, misnamed treaties, in which they assumed exclusive right of purchasing at fixed prices all available produce and declared themselves free of all duties and taxes . . . Under the guns of their forts, they purchased, if such term can be applied, whatever they desired of the produce of the country and the articles imported for sale by the neighbouring traders, giving in return . . . whatever they were pleased to consider a fit equivalent. In this way cargoes of the richest description, which sold in Europe at enormous prices were obtained here at almost nominal cost. Factories were found along the shores of Sumatra, the Malayan Peninsula, Java, Borneo, Celebes, Moluccas and ports thus dealt with, if unfortunately they were unable to expel the intruders, were rapidly reduced to ruin, native traders ceased to frequent them, and the Europeans, finding them no longer profitable, left them.

In fact, according to Braddell, it was the "gross injustice and oppression" of the European powers that was largely responsible for the decline of the Malay society. As the author again aptly surmised (page 327), "the system of trading under the guns of fortified factories . . . must be considered as the cause of most, if not all, of the evils which followed, evils which continue to depress these countries below the position they are entitled to hold in the scale of nations . . .". Apart from the impoverishment and destruction of the native economy, these ruthless policies also resulted in a breakdown of constituted authority and the rise of anarchy, for "the Europeans satisfied themselves with the acquisition of sufficient authority to procure commodities. They were at no pains to supply the want of that regulated authority which their presence disturbed and which is necessary to the existence of nations. Universal anarchy prevailed (page 335)." The elimination of this major source of economic activity also drove the chiefs to piracy, apparently the only "natural recourse" available (page 328).[1]

Alatas, in his book *The Myth of The Lazy Native*, also provides an insightful analysis of the role of these European powers in the gradual pauperization and degeneration of the Malay Archipelago, including the Malay Peninsula. Restrictive treaties imposed by the Dutch, and to some extent, the Portuguese, repressed the perpetuation and development of free trade and arrested the continued economic well-being and prosperity of these nations. So repressive were these agreements that, Alatas states (1977: 196), "even the fowls of Naning were coveted by the company." Furthermore, some of these treaties also prevented the right of states like Johore and Perak to trade with foreign traders. Similarly, Pahang and Trengganu were also imposed with 'agreements' which had the effect of restricting available markets for their sale of their products such as wool and silk (page 194). Selangor also suffered the same fate (page 195). So extensive was the impact of these restrictions that, as Alatas remarked (page 196), "In the course of the 17th and 18th centuries, the Dutch had succeeded in bringing about hundreds of such restrictive agreements with the indigenous chiefs and rulers throughout the entire region from Malacca to Ternate."

It must be pointed out that the British too contributed to the gradual impoverishment of Malay society. They were not averse to the Dutch monopoly system in places where it proved to be remunerative. For instance, in 1801, the British Resident signed a treaty with the Penghulu of Naning, Abdul Said, the effect of which ensured that all the latter's tin had to be supplied to the English East India Company at a fixed rate. In addition, the inhabitants had to abstain from all commercial intercourse with the foreign nations and towns other than Malacca (Muller: 79). Likewise, in 1800 Kedah was bound not to admit other Europeans into any part of her territory (page 79). The British also prudently secured access to the Peninsula and other places before Malacca was restored to the Netherlands. In 1818, Perak, Selangor and Johore had to sign agreements not to exclude or hamper British trade by treaties with other nations (page 80).

[1] On the adverse effects of colonial policies on the general well-being of other societies, please see Frantz Fanon (1963); Van Der Kolff (1929); and W.F. Wertheim (1956: Chapter 5).

Such measures certainly served to restrict and arrest the free development of trade in the interests of the Malay states. Together with the ruthless policies of the Dutch, they were mainly responsible for the poverty and anarchic conditions of Malay society, as Raffles had witnessed later. Raffles himself must have been aware of these gross injustices. Yet he chose to highlight the problem of the decline of the Malays as one due primarily to its existing system of laws without taking into consideration these crucial historical factors, which hampered legal growth and which contributed much to the decline of the society. Such an evaluation is superficial and misleading, to say the least.

Raffles' allegation is also inadequate in explaining the continued prosperity of the Malay states prior to the coming of the Europeans into the region. Before the European powers had a foothold in the region, the Malay states enjoyed the prosperity of a well-developed and established system of commerce with extensive international trading links. Thus in 1518, Duarte Barbossa observed that the city of Malacca was the richest seaport with the greatest number of wholesale merchants and abundance of shipping and trade in the whole world (Duncan, 1921, 2: 175). Kedah was also mentioned as a country "where there were many great ships." According to the author this was a place where Moorish ships came hither yearly from diverse regions (pages 164–65). Such a developed system of trade and commerce would surely have been inconceivable without a regular and defined system of commercial, civil and criminal laws, contrary to that deduced by Raffles (1835: 91–2).

Furthermore, direct accounts of the infrastructure provided by the laws of the Malays were also revealed in the records of the Portuguese traveller Tome Pires (Cortesao, 1944, 2: 229) in his *Suma Oriental*, the validity of whose account "is gathered from what the majority affirm". At Malacca, Pires described the existence of established commercial customs which effectively determined the prices and sale of goods in an orderly, fair and efficient manner (page 273).

> It is an old custom he said, that as soon as the merchants arrive, they unload the cargo and pay their dues or present . . . ten or twenty merchants gathered together with the owner of the merchandise and bid for it and by the said merchants the price was fixed and divided amongst them all in proportion. And because time was short and the merchandise considerable, the merchants were cleared and then those of Malacca took to Malacca the merchandise to their ships and sold

> them at their pleasure; for which the traders received their settlement and gains and the local merchants made profits. And through this custom, the land lived in an orderly way and they carried on their business. And this was done thus orderly so that they did not favour the merchant from the ship, nor did he go away displeased; for the law and the prices of merchandise in Malacca are well known.

Apart from Malacca, Pires also noted that Pahang, a tributary of Malacca, was a good city having a good port with many merchants trading in merchandise (page 263). Had an established and regular system of laws been absent, the successful commercial development of the city could not have occurred. In addition, the author also mentioned neighbouring lands inhabited by Malays such as Klang, Kuala Kesang, Selangor, Bruas and Perak. These settlements, according to him, had criminal and civil jurisdiction in their lands (pages 259–61). Such an assertion implies the existence of a stable and regulated system of government dealing with essential aspects of social life.

These historical sources serve to show that Malay laws could not have been primarily responsible, let alone responsible, for the degeneration of Malay society. Furthermore, these sources reveal that it was the coming of the Europeans and the exploitative effects of European commercial capitalism that contributed much to the decline of Malay society.

Raffles' attempts at portraying the shortcomings of the substantive aspects of Malay law are also marred by unfounded claims. A clear instance is revealed in his perception that the civil destruction and general unrest plaguing Malay society stemmed from the absence of clearly defined rules regulating political succession. Thus, he asserted (1835: 93):

> the want of a well-defined rule of succession to the government in the families of the Malay Raja is constantly productive of innumerable parties, division and civil agitations in every state. This however is an evil common to all governments where the Mohammedan religion prevails though its evils are mostly felt in comparatively rude state of society, such as exists in the Malay countries. This evil was prevented effectually during the Dutch domination by their assuming the paramount right of granting investiture to every prince who succeeded to the government of a country; and if such a plan as I have alluded to, were to be adopted by the English, a similar policy, either by granting investiture or by recognizing the heir apparent, would naturally require to be followed. A regulation of the kind, I have utmost reason

> for thinking, would be highly acceptable to all the Malay nations: for among a great number of them, at present, the death of a prince is regarded with horror by all his subjects as the signal for intestine war, ruin and devastation.

Raffles' suggestion that unrest and instability are caused by the lack of a defined rule of political succession is erroneous. Such a fundamental aspect of Malay life could not have escaped the ambit of the law. Pires, for instance, explicitly noted (Cortesao, 1944, 2: 265) the existence of such a defined law in Malacca, as follows:

> The rule in Malacca is that if the king has an elder son by his wife, he marries him at fifteen years of age or later; and if the said son has a son or daughter by his wife, so that the king has a grandson, he relinquishes the government and the son remains in possession of the kingdom and the father is no longer king. However, he is respected as before, though he does not govern.

Apart from this historical record, it is inconceivable that Malay feudal society, which ascribed to the sovereign the fountain of authority, should not ensure the maintenance of the status quo by an acknowledged and defined system of regulation. Historically, it was also the existence of an established rule of succession that entrenched the dynasty at Malacca (Hooker, 1970: 78).[2]

Succession problems generally arose due to a violation of established rules by various factions of the Malay ruling class. In their quest for power and authority, warring interest groups gathered the support of powerful parties to ensure their choice of the claimant to the throne irrespective of the law of succession. A clear instance in Malay history is provided by the usurpation of the throne by Sultan Mahmud Shah, the last ruler of Malacca, due to the support gathered by the powerful influence of his grandfather, the Bendahara and his associates of court mandarins. It was the power conflict between these opposing factions that brought about civil strife and unrest.

Such instances of usurpation, despite established laws of succession, also occurred in medieval English history. The law of primogeniture did not guarantee the prevention of unrest caused by rival kingmakers of nobles and gentry. The war of Roses in the 15th century,

---

[2] As example, please see "Ninety-Nine Laws of Perak" in *Readings in Malay Adat Laws*, ed. M.B. Hooker, Singapore University Press, Singapore 1970, p. 78.

a faction fight between families allied to the royal house contending for power and possession of the crown, is but one instance of a series of such exploits in violation of the law (Trevelyan, 1926: 263).

Attempts at portraying Malay adat laws as devoid of sound humanitarian values are weak due to inaccurate conceptions of the law. Such perceptions are revealed in the discussion on Malay adat law governing debtors. Crawford, for instance, attempts to convey that such laws are oppressive by asserting the following (1967: 97–8):

> If a debtor is unable to pay his creditor, he is compelled to serve him until the debt be discharged and he is then nearly in the condition of a slave. Every man has his fixed price, and if the debt exceeds this, he either loses his liberty altogether or his family is compelled to serve the creditor along with him.

Crawford's view must be subjected to several qualifications and corrections, when examined in the light of the Malay legal digests. The *Malacca Legal Code* (*Undang-Undang Melaka*), for instance, clearly provides for the protection of the rights of the debtor's family in the event of the failure of payment of a debt. Thus the law stipulates:

> "Concerning debtors who have wives and children: the husband alone enters the service (of the creditor) even though the debt is the common responsibility of the husband and his wife and children; the wife and children do not enter the service . . . should (the husband) die . . . it is not permissible to let (the burden of repaying) the debt fall on them, but (the debt) will be divided into three parts, one third is to be paid by the debtor's wife and children, two thirds are lost (by the creditor). Such is the law (Liaw, 1976: 169)."
>
> Furthermore, if the wives and children are ignorant of the debts, it is not permissible to demand payment from them. Only if they acknowledge the debt and there are witnesses, is it permissible to do so (pages 167–69). The law also protects the debtor from abuse by laying down the rule that "with regard to people who are in debt, however long (the debt has remained unpaid), the creditor can only claim the double amount according to custom (page 167)."[3]

[3] It is perhaps also relevant to mention the differences between the condition and position of slaves and debt bondsmen in Southeast Asian societies from those of the West. This will provide a more comprehensive picture of the effects of Malay laws relating to slavery and debt bondage. Alatas explains this in the following words (1977: 210–11): "Slavery in Southeast Asia has a different connotation from that in the West. Generally speaking, a slave in Southeast Asia was a domestic help or a farm assistant integrated into the family organization. The cruel treatment of slaves found in the West Indies and the United States before, had never characterised the Southeast Asian institution of slavery. Before the coming of the foreigners, both

Attempts at portraying Malay adat laws as lacking humanitarian values are based on erroneous allegations contrary to the spirit and letter of the laws. A clear instance is revealed in Crawford's evaluation of the Malay penal laws. We have seen in Chapter One that Crawford (1967: 104–5) condemned these laws, referring to them as "arbitrary violence" showing "little regard for human life". "Death", according to Crawford, "is the punishment for a hundred trifling offences and is awarded with a wantonness which shocks the humanity of civilisation." Crawford fails to perceive that, as in any civilized society, Malay adat laws are characterized by a central set of right and wrong forms of conduct, corresponding to which is a gradation of punishment. Take for instance, the *Malacca Legal Code* (*Undang-Undang Melaka*), a legal digest that Crawford uses in support of his claims.

Contrary to Crawford's allegations, we find that in the Code, the death sentence is imposed only in the event of the commission of certain grave offences. Apart from those relating to the violation of rulers' prerogatives, murder, stabbing, slashing, causing grievous hurt, robbery, forging and counterfeiting the royal seal, defying royal commands, and rape are perhaps the main offences upon which capital punishments were imposed (Liaw, 1976: 69, 167). These wrongs can hardly be regarded as "trifling". In his study of the legal codes of France, Austria, Germany, Russia and Italy and their development from pre medieval era to the first half of the twentieth century, the prominent social scientist Sorokin, discovered that many similar wrongdoings found in these societies were regarded as absolute crimes. Like the offences defined in Malay laws, they included murder, bodily injury, blows and violence, insult, theft, plunder, unlawful appropriation of another's property, robbery, rape and attempts against the supreme organs of state (Sorokin, 1937–41, vol. 2: 557).

Apart from the death sentence imposed on these specified offences, Malay laws imposed milder forms of punishments on a multitude of wrongs. These included the impositions of fines, the amount of which varied according to the nature of the offence. In the Malacca Legal Code, fines were imposed for the stealing of agricultural produce

Oriental and European, the main sources of recruitment of slaves had been war and incurred debts. After the coming of the Europeans with their towns and trading posts, the slaves developed into a commercial commodity, an article of export. Organized slave raids increased as the main source of recruitment, accompanied by an increase of inhuman treatment".

(Liaw, 1976: 81), domestic animals (page 83) and Malay clippers called *perahu* (page 81). Fines were also imposed on those who harboured runaway slaves (page 87) and the striking of slaves by freemen (page 75). Lower down the scale of gravity of offences, only compensation is demanded, such as in cases which include the destruction of borrowed property (page 145), the sale of defective goods (page 141), breach of agreement to deliver goods (page 123–25), negligence (pages 117, 147), and many other types of wrongs. These diverse forms of punishment were meted out in relation to the gravity of offences, as perceived by the society, reveal Crawford's hasty generalizations.

Even the death sentence for offences mentioned earlier can be mitigated, albeit subject to several pertinent qualifications. One instance is in the case where the offender may have been provoked to commit the offence or the killing is carried out because the arms of the law do not reach far enough and the failure to act immediately may result in more harmful consequences. These exceptions are conveyed in the relevant articles of the *Malacca Legal Code* which states that a murderer may be pardoned if he kills one of the following: 1. a paramour, 2. a ruffian who cannot be arrested and is dangerous, 3. thieves who cannot be captured, 4. a person who brings disgrace to others, for instance (by) slapping someone or by any other humiliating action if the case has not reached the minister (pages 69–71).

Apart from these defined exceptions, the punishment for murder is death. The severity of the punishment for this offence reveals the foolhardiness of Crawford's statement that: "It is remarkable that there is not, in any language of the Indian islanders, words equivalent to ours to murder, or murderer; no terms which express the horror which we attach to these. In these tongues, to murder is simply 'to kill', and the murderer is no more than 'one who kills (Crawford, 1967: 124)'". If human life were indeed of such little value to these societies, as Crawford strongly suggested, there would have been no reason to legalize capital punishment for murder. The harsh punishment relating to this offence by itself reveals that the protection and preservation of human life was a fundamental value upheld by the society.

Indignation and contempt for some of these laws also arise from a failure to consider their positive object and purpose. Thus, Crawford expressed disgust (page 121) for laws that allow for an individual to engage the services of hirelings in settling disputes with a wrongdoer with the knowledge of the judge. Crawford implied that the acknowledgement of the judge undermined the impartiality of the legal system. His discontentment stemmed from his failure to perceive that such an arrangement is founded on the basis that the right of redress should not be abused or carried out improperly. The requirement by law of the judges' knowledge prior to the commission of the act reveals recognition for control and constraint and the desire for the protection of life and liberty. As the *Malacca Legal Code* stipulates (Liaw, 1976: 101):

> With regard to rules governing people who hire (a man) to beat someone without the knowledge of the judge, he the hirer shall be fined . . . because he is held negligent in failing to inform the judge. That is also to enable the judge to continuously uphold royal authority . . . Such is the law that is being administered by the judge in the country . . . in order that the common people may be protected.

The purpose of the law being to obtain redress and to ensure that justice was done, is again clearly revealed in the following legal provision (page 101): ". . . If a man hires someone with the knowledge of the judge, he shall incur no fine . . . because the person so beaten was guilty of Judah, i.e., he insulted others indiscriminately and was quarrelsome in public . . .".

Discontentment with the laws also arose from the fact that they allowed for hired men to settle disputes. However, Crawford failed to take into consideration the fact that, in a society where there is an absence of an elaborate law-enforcing machinery comprising staff specially employed to fulfil the task of complementing the judgments of the court in securing redress, to which Crawford was probably accustomed, resolution of disputes must lie either with one's kin or members of the society paid for the task. Though the means employed differed from those commonly known to the author, it does not justify his assumption that the law lacked sound values.

In fact, the practice of the private enforcement of redress is not unique to Malay society only. In medieval European history, particularly during the feudal era, this method of enforcement of law as evident in the vendetta was but a common and pervasive means whereby injury or death was avenged. Such a mode of ensuring redress was carried out with the knowledge of judges (Bloch, 1978: 126–28). Due to the prevalence of strong ties of blood relationship, the moral obligation to avenge a wrong lay heavily with the kin. The solitary individual could do but little (page 126). As the renowned jurist Pound noted, within the political organization of such societies in European history, internal order of the kin group was maintained by discipline. A clash of interests would lead to self-help and private war, thus the staple institution of the society was the blood feud. It was the regulation of self-help and private war that characterized such societies. Only later did law develop to restrain private war and suppress individual revenge (Pound, 1944: 41–7). Crawford's hasty evaluative generalizations of Malay values and its humanity is clearly ahistorical and asociological. The modern English system of administration of justice formed the yardstick upon which he pronounced the values of the Malays and their humanity without taking into consideration the conditions of the society he was examining.

Sweeping generalizations without the support of adequate or relevant data also mar Crawford's study. For instance, Crawford simply asserts (1967: 114) as a matter of course that "theft and robbery" were naturally the most frequent of all crimes among people where the "protection afforded by law or government is so inadequate." Such pejorative allegations were made without an iota of evidence. Crawford's characteristic denunciation of the laws is also flawed by prejudicial stereotypes, as depicted in his assertion, for instance (page 96), that "loans, as in other rude states of society, where neither law nor morals encourage integrity in commercial transactions are usually made on pledges."

Even sound ethical principles embodied in the law are dismissed as but a reflection of the primitive state of society. For instance, Crawford criticized legal provisions that require persons involved in litigation to uphold standards of fairness, probity and impartiality. He dismissed these (1967: 85) as "self-evident maxims and crude instructions" which could have only been "paraded in a very rude and early stage of social union, and of the science of ethics." Perhaps Crawford was unaware of the fact that even modern English law contains such essential legal principles. A pertinent instance is found in the rules of natural justice, which regulate minimum standards of fairness. The principle stipulates that firstly, an adjudicator must not have any direct financial or proprietary interest in the outcome of the proceeding of cases in which he presides, and secondly, he must not be reasonably suspected to or show a real likelihood of bias (De Smith and Brazier 1989: 558–61). These rules clearly mean that adjudicators must dispense justice in a manner that is impartial and objective. The values found in Malay laws also reveal these positive traits. Yet Crawford chose to weave negative connotations into these laws.

Furthermore, his evaluation that the institutions of government defined in the laws of Southeast Asian societies reveal their primitive state, is confusing. He asserted that "as in all rude periods of society, the chief, lord, king or sovereign under whatever name recognized, administers the law. In smaller communities, he does so in person; in the larger ones by delegate. The administration of the law is, in fact, but a subordinate branch of executive government, conducted by one and the same hands" (Crawford, 1967: 79).

Crawford's remarks imply that the Malay adat laws regulating distribution of functions of government differ from those of more advanced societies. Yet, the argument is puzzling when a comparison is made with the relevant English law which, needless to say, Crawford would not consider to be "rude". In English legal history, the sovereign, who is not above the law, recognizes and administers it. Furthermore, Ministers are delegated with powers that are exercised for and on behalf of the sovereign. The Act of Settlement, for instance, clearly states that ". . . all the Kings and Queens who shall ascend the throne of this realm ought to administer the government . . . according to the said laws; and their officers and Ministers ought to serve them respectively according to the same" (Wade and Bradley, 1965: 179). Moreover, the administration of the law has generally been part of the functions of the executive (Wade and Bradley, 1965, part 1).

An extension of his ethnocentric attitude is also revealed in his evaluation of the arrangement of the laws. According to the author, "all of them display a character of rudeness and barbarism . . . no attempt is made in them at arrangement and classification but the most incompatible matters are blended together and forms of judicature, criminal and civil jurisprudence, maxims of morality and commercial regulations are incongruously intermixed" (Crawford, 1967: 78–9). Crawford's framework of reference, which is certainly that of English law, prevents him from evaluating objectively the unique character of Malay laws. He fails to perceive the historically and socially specific conditions within which they originated. For instance, English criminal law as distinct from civil law (in so far as the sovereign is in all cases the prosecuting party) developed in relation to the growth of the power of the sovereign in Western society during the Middle Ages (Cherry, 1890: 103).

Crawford's judgmental evaluation of Malay laws is a parochial one. He visualized law as none other than a body of rules, distinct from morality, and internally coherent and comprehensive, divided into the major segments of constitutional law, civil law and criminal law. Seeing that Malay laws did not fall within this common category, Crawford concluded that they were barbaric and not harmonious. Such a conception reveals a lack of objectivity in grasping the unique historical specifications of Malay adat laws, which may throw light on the understanding of the nature of the law. As Van Vollenhoven, the Dutch scholar on Indonesian adat law, aptly remarked, "viewed through the eyes of a codist, the legal inventory of the Indies presents a jumble, an incomplete, inadequate and untidy whole; but when explored by one whose desire for knowledge and explanation of the living law on earth is inspired by the very diversity of its past and present manifestations, this same inventory becomes an inexhaustible source of instruction" (Vollenhoven, 1981: 1–2).

Contextually, the writings of Crawford and Raffles coincided with the period of industrial capitalism in Europe. There was an increasing need to provide raw materials required by the industries back home and to establish foreign markets by which "surplus" products could be exported. The fortified trading bases, which had profitably served European commerce and held off competitors in the region, were gradually giving way to the need for a more settled producing and consuming area. Colonial capitalism had by this time become firmly entrenched in the Malay Peninsula. This form of capitalism was characterized by the following traits (a) predominant control and access to capital by an alien economic power; (b) the control of the colony by a government run by members of the alien power, acting on its behalf; (c) the highest level of business, trade and industry, held by the alien dominating community; (d) direction of the country's export and import trade to suit the interest of the alien ruling power; (e) a bias towards the agrarian mode of production as opposed to that of industry; (f) the minimal expansion of technological and scientific skills; (g) the organization of production around semi-free labour; (h) absence of guilds or trade unions as a counter weight to exploitation; (i) non-involvement of large sections of the population in direct capitalist enterprise; (j) presence of a set of antitheses in the colonized societies described by the term "dualism" (Alatas, 1977: 2).

Examined in this context, the attempts by the writers at consistently undermining Malay adat laws may have been conditioned by the ideological interests of the colonial power to justify the maintenance and perpetuation of their influence in the Malay Peninsula. As Alatas (1977: 1), in thc introduction of his work *The Myth of the Lazy Native* explains, ideology is a system of belief characterized by the following traits: a) it seeks to justify a particular political, social and economic order, b) in this attempt it distorts that part of social reality likely to contradict its main presuppositions, c) it exists primarily in the form of thought content which is different from its latent content, d) it is authoritative in nature, e) it expresses the interests of a distinct group, f) when it is dominant it creates a false consciousness among the group it represents as well as the group it dominates, g) it can draw its ideas from any source, science, religion, culture, economics, history, etc., h) it arises out of conflicting interests of separate groups in a society with a pronounced division of labour and social classes and i) its major ideas are eventually to a large extent conditioned by the mode of production in a given time and place. The negative portrayal of the adat is but part of a wider ideological scheme aimed at denigrating the image of the Malays and their institutions in order to rationalize European conquest and control.

By the twentieth century, these developments were already in full swing. Further large-scale territorial advances were made by the British. It was also during this period that the system of indirect political rule introduced by the British was already firmly entrenched. By virtue of this system, native states and institutions were to be preserved as far as possible under close European supervision, so that the Malays could be more conveniently governed through the agency of their own traditional leaders operating within the traditional institutional framework as modified to suit European needs (Emerson, 1964: 7). This system of indirect rule served as a moral justification for the perpetuation of European dominance by laying claim to being the means by which the British could lead the "backward" people to progress, preserving the best of the old and integrating it with the best of the new. The conceptions of law as found in the writings of Wilkinson and Winstedt cannot be comprehensively and effectively understood without taking into consideration these broader economic and political concerns.

Consistent with the policy of preserving indigenous institutions, which suited British colonial interest, their writings reveal conscious attempts at selecting and preserving what they conceived as the more "civilized" and "advanced" traits of the Malay law. These positive traits, as we have seen in Chapter One, were attributed to the adat Perpateh, a term the authors utilized to refer to the customs found in the matrilineal societies of certain districts in Negri Sembilan and the northern areas of the state of Malacca. (Bador, 1963: 10–11).[4] As opposed to this, they severely denigrated the adat Temenggong, the custom of the other peninsular states. In doing so, they distorted the image of these laws. Not only was the adat Temenggong misconceived, even the perception of the adat Perpateh was erroneous in many essential aspects.

The conception of the adat Perpateh found in the writing of Wilkinson, for instance, reveals a static image of Malay laws. The following assertion illustrates this point: "It was a simple homely law of which its votaries were always proud. It was reverenced as a priceless possession; it was never to be amended or altered: Di-anjak layu, di-aleh mati. Uprooted it withers; moved it dies" (Hooker, 1970: 30).[5]

The interpretation of this provision is erroneous. In effect, the provision conveys that a living adat is one that is "rooted" in the social context in which it originates and evolves. When it is removed from its context, its dynamism and relevance in fulfilling the requirements of the society ceases. The saying has no bearing on the issue of change or modification of the adat. Furthermore, Malays have never conceived law as an absolutely changeless phenomenon. They have long recognized that laws which become obsolete as a result of changes in social conditions must gradually sink into oblivion and make way for new ones. Such an understanding of the dynamic

---

[4] Abdul Kahar Bador details the principal areas in Negri Sembilan in which the adat Perpateh was operative. These included the four major *luak* (the traditional socio-political and territorial unit), namely, Luak Sungei Ujong, Luak Jelebu, Luak Rembau and Luak Johol.

[5] This saying also occurs in the collection by Caldecott, A., "Jelebu Customary Songs and Saying", *JSBRAS*, No. 78, June 1918, p. 36.

nature of law is evident in the *Undang-Undang Sungei Ujong*. Article 12 of this digest, which is instructive and pertinent, is as follows: "Each time the tide runs high, the rivers' banks changes; each time there are new rulers, the custom changes" (Winstedt and de Jong, 1954: 42).[6] This article strongly conveys an important attribute of the adat namely its ability to modify and adjust to suit changing conditions.

Support for this view is also evident in the opinions of Dutch adat law scholars. As Van Vollenhoven surmised (1981: 24):

> Adat law is not (as has been assumed only too often by Europeans), something immutable, though changes in it are not normally visible within the period of observation granted to a single observer. On the contrary, it has been confirmed from various sources that 'local' usage gradually adjusts itself to changing needs' (Snouck Hurgronje, 1894: 353); that the adat 'changes with the generations' and remains static 'for hardly a single moment' (1893: 910); that the passage of time and contact with neighbouring peoples made deep inroads upon it' (Willer, 1846:6) and that 'however invariable the character of adat law may appear to be, it does in fact adjust itself to changing conditions, though gradually, and therefore slowly, with the result that this (process) almost escapes observation, unless suddenly an opportunity presents itself to cast an eye upon the situation of a century ago' (Liefrinck, 1890: 328). It is therefore a fallacy to assume that the 'native adat is an unchanging whole, not subject to the laws of history'.

Van Vollenhoven's observations are relevant in throwing light upon this aspect of adat law because of two essential reasons. The author's perception is based upon an earlier discussion of the Minangkabau adat Perpateh maxim of Sumatra which is itself similar to Article 12 of the *Undang-Undang Sungei Ujong* mentioned above (page 24). Furthermore, it is generally acknowledged that, broadly speaking, the Minangkabau of the Malay Peninsula share a common origin with those of Indonesia. Hence, there is a close connection of the adat within Indonesia to the customary traditions and laws of the Minangkabau of the Malay Peninsula (Ter Haar, 1948: 1).

---

[6] This is a Malay legal digest from Sungei Ujong in Negeri Sembilan, selected provisions of which were utilized by Wilkinson in his description and evaluation of the adat Perpateh. I am aware that Hooker, in his article (1968), A note on the Malayan legal digest, JMBRAS, vol. 41, part 1: 158–159, categorised this digest as having relevance to the adat Temenggong. Nevertheless, his opinion is unsubstantiated since Hooker did not provide any basis in support of his view.

While the flexible nature of the adat is clear, it is also pertinent to note that the law stipulates clearly the constancy of sound values and principles. These include amongst others, fairness, justice, probity, and propriety. They are regarded as "*chupak yang asali*" (ideal standards), the permanent attribute of which is revealed in the following phrase: "*Itulah chupak, yang tiada lengkang dipanas, yang tiada lapok oleh hujan. Setapak tiada lalu, setapak tiada surut*" (Winstedt and De Jong, 1954: 41). That is the scale which is not worn by heat, nor weathered by rain. It does not advance a step, nor does it retire a step. The existence of these essential traits of permanence and change, the requisite of any living and dynamic legal system is certainly evident in the adat Perpateh. Yet Wilkinson chooses to convey an image of the adat which is static.

An extension of the static image of the adat Perpateh can also be discerned in Winstedt's writing. By asserting that the adat Perpateh was "safe in the keeping of democracy of inland agriculturalists, impervious to foreign influence", Winstedt (1953: 98–99) fails to perceive that the adat as in the case of any other living legal system dynamically accommodates forces of change. Leaving aside the influence of Islam, an issue that will be dealt with in the following chapter, Winstedt's conception reveals a failure to take into account the constant impact of other social forces in the gradual development of the adat. For instance in his book, *Indonesian Sociological Studies*, Schrieke (1957: 107) attributes changes in the adat land laws of the Minangkabau communities in the nineteenth century to changes in the society's economic foundation.

Schrieke addressed the issue as follows (page 142):

> Unquestionably the organization of Minangkabau community even now rests on the traditional basis and Minangkabau society moves within the framework of adat. But this must not blind us to the fact that natural social forces are unceasingly busy undermining that basis, labouring to make the framework fall to pieces. The outer appearance of social forms must not mislead us. The 'closed production economy', the economic foundations of ancient customary social system, had had its day. The undivided family property is crumbling to pieces under the pressure exercised by the money economy. Land tenure is growing less certain; economic differentiation is increasing. Restrictions laid down by tradition are becoming an embarrassment. Hence any effort to force this society back into its old grooves artificially is doomed to failure from the very outset.

The Adat Perpateh areas in the Malay Peninsula were similarly exposed to these forces of change (de Jong, 1960: 165–66).[7] Winstedt, in failing to take into consideration these inevitable influences on the adat Perpateh, reflects his static conception of the law. Such an understanding of the adat is disastrous, for the relevance of any legal system depends on its ability to adjust to and accommodate changing conditions.

In fact, it can be said that the writers' perception of the adat as the pure law of the Malays, untainted by change is reminiscent of the views of the body of colonial legal writings such as that of Jones, whose works reveal the assumption that there was historically, in India, a body of laws and codes that had been fixed from time immemorial. Such a conception is not only misleading, it also distorts reality. However, these authors did not succumb to similar notions of English law. English case law was historically derived, based on the finding of precedent and constantly evolving. It was, as Cohn submits, perceived as flexible and above all subject to multiple interpretations by judges and lawyers, responsive to history and change. But Oriental law differed drastically. It was unchanging and unchangeable and if there were differences in interpretation, these arose out of ignorance or venality of the Oriental legal scholars (Cohn, 1996: 71). More significantly, these scholars were of the view that it is this pure law that must be preserved. In effect, however, such attempts at preservation of the law fossilizes it, thereby rendering it irrelevant.

The writers' portrayal of the adat Perpateh as the true law of the Malays also reveals a naive perception of the nature of law. Wilkinson's following description is a case in point (Hooker, 1970: 8): "These sayings are a great power in the Minangkabau states; being known to all and having the full force of public opinion behind them, reference to them is sufficient to compel even an unjust judge to do justice to the litigants before him." Such a notion of willing acquiescence to the adat laws is unrealistic. After all, it cannot be denied that law is essentially a means of control and constraint. Law imposes liabilities, duties and restrictions. To assume that these are accepted willingly reveals a failure to take into consideration the compelling

[7] The effects of some of these factors on the Minangkabau communities and their laws in the Malay Peninsula are highlighted by P.E. de Josselin de Jong, 1960. *Minangkabau and Negri Sembilan*. Djakarta: Bhratara, 165–66.

nature of law. Furthermore, if every member of the community fully supports the adat Perpateh, why then is there need for legal sanctions? Although undeniably most men obey laws irrespective of these sanctions, nevertheless, their existence serves to show that there are turbulent elements in society that oppose and violate the laws (Malinowski, 1966: 13).

As opposed to the admiration and reverence for the adat Perpateh, the writers, as we have seen in Chapter One, denigrated the image of the adat Temenggong. Wilkinson, for instance, claims (Hooker, 1970: 9–10) that the adat Perpateh is "mild", "democratic", "lenient to first offenders", "always ready to condone a wrong", while the latter is "autocratic", "brutal", "cruel" and "harsh". Many of these evaluations refer to variations in the laws regulating punishment found in these two legal systems. Such evaluative comparisons are wanting. The authors failed to appreciate the problems involved in comparing these laws that operated within different social milieu. Avoiding the salient features that set them apart and how they affect the adat results in misleading and fallacious judgments. As Ter Haar (1948: 46) had pointed out, "not infrequently, superficial comparison of legal institutions or rules of law that have been removed from their context has been tried but it always leads to misunderstanding and frequently to misuse of the facts."

It has been systematically demonstrated by Sorokin (1937–41: 595) that the amount and severity of laws relating to wrongs, in particular the penal laws of a given society can only be understood upon bases other than the letter of the law. Sorokin viewed the harshness of laws as determined by what he calls the heterogeneous or homogenous ethico-juridical conviction of the members of the society. He sought to establish that the greater the heterogeneity of this mentality, the more severe the punishment. Conversely, the more homogenous the mentality, the milder the laws. A homogenous ethico-juridical mentality, according to Sorokin, is characterized by shared or common socio-cultural values and a unified network of social relationships. On the contrary, a heterogeneous one is characterized by diversity of the value system and the absence of a unified network of relationships (pages 596–98).

In the case of the former, punishments are relatively mild, as crimes do not pose a threat to the society due to a "collective morality" and strong social ties. In the latter situation, however, the "revitalised" system of values and weak social relationships necessitates the imposition of harsher laws in order to maintain social cohesion and prevent conflicts (pages 598–99).

These essential principles are relevant in throwing light on the differences in severity of punishment found in the Malay legal systems. Applying Sorokin's thesis, the relative severity of adat Temenggong laws on punishment as compared to the adat Perpateh can only be effectively understood if such evaluative comparisons take into consideration factors other than the letter of the law. The relative harshness of the laws of the adat Temenggong, as in the case of the Malacca Legal Code (*Undang-Undang Melaka*), for instance, must be examined in relation to the social milieu in which these laws originated and developed. Historically, the population of the seaport of Malacca was a plural and heterogeneous one comprising a large number of traders, missionaries and adventurers from many parts of Asia. An indication of the extent of the multiplicity of the ethnic groups found in Malacca is provided in the records of Pires. According to Pires, "in the port of Malacca, very often eighty-four languages have been found spoken, every one distinct, as the inhabitants of Malacca affirm; and this in Malacca alone" (Cortesao, 1944: 269).

Apart from the Malays, the dominant majority included Indian communities, both Hindu and Muslim, Javanese, Chinese, Arabs and many others. Though some of these social groups were assimilated into the indigenous society, for instance through marriage, as is the case with a number of Arabs, Tamils and Parsees, the remaining retained their ethnic and cultural identity. These latter groups, it has been said, "comprised a mosaic of social worlds which touched but did not interpenetrate (Sandhu and Wheatley, 1983: 542–46)." They accorded ethnic loyalties to their compatriots rather than the city of Malacca. The coexistence of all these diverse groups bound by the objective of profiting from the trade of the country while sharing little else in common found its effect on the laws. The relative severity of the laws is required to ensure the peaceful maintenance of the cosmopolitan society. Sorokin's thesis would presumably apply to the other adat Temenggong states other than Malacca, since they are equally, if not more diverse in their social composition. Gullick, in his study of the social structure of the Western Malay states including Perak, Selangor, Pahang and Kedah prior to 1875, noted that, except in Negri Sembilan, the village population in these states was very heterogeneous in terms of descent, kinship and culture. Due to their diversity, they did not even have any natural alignment into larger groups other than the villages (Gullick, 1965: 43).

The situation, however, differs in the adat Perpateh areas. In the case of Negri Sembilan for instance, migrants from Minangkabau who settled here in the sixteenth century succeeded in extending their value system, their social and political institutions to the waris or the heirs of the country. The latter assimilated and absorbed these cultural conventions and laws that the migrants had brought along with them. Furthermore, a unified network of social relationships, the vestiges of a system of alignment based on the matrilineal descent that had originated in Minangkabau were brought by the immigrants and became established (Gullick, 1958: 37–42). Thus instead of the existence of diverse social groups, each maintaining its own distinctive cultural identity and values as found in the adat Temenggong area of Malacca, the conditions of the adat Perpateh areas may not have necessitated the existence of relatively harsh penal measures.

The writers also neglected taking into account the social milieu of the adat Temenggong while they consciously did so in the case of the adat Perpateh. Thus Wilkinson asserted (Hooker, 1970: 9, 14): "In the Negri Sembilan life was largely communal. Imprisonment and mutilation such as the lopping off of a limb rendered a man a burden to the community instead of an aid." Furthermore, he noted: "The communal system explains both why the law was humane and why it could afford to be humane." In the same way, Winstedt remarked: "Life in a clan is communal so the death penalty, imprisonment and mutilation involved the loss of a pair of hands to the tribe. Hence the Minangkabau punishment for crime except in the case of heinous and incorrigible offenders, always took the form of restitution" (Winstedt, 1956: 93).

This neglect in analysing the adat Temenggong in relation to the conditions of the society may have been a conscious one for the authors did not fail to utilise this argument in their evaluation of English law. Thus when it came to explaining the relative harshness of English law in comparison with the adat Perpateh, Winstedt provided the following justification: "With a rigidity unavoidable in law designed for a large population, British law sentences murderers to death and cares nothing for tribal loss or for compensation in the shape of fowls, goats and sisters' son" (Winstedt, 1953: 99). Such an argument however, was not extended to the adat Temenggong.

This attitude of partiality towards the adat Temenggong is also revealed in attempts at distracting interest in studying it even at the expense of inconsistency in reasoning. Hence referring to this adat, Wilkinson remarked; "Yet, in a sense, it is supposed to represent progress. It led to a higher material civilisation; it developed class distinctions and court life; it brought new blood and new ideas into Malaya; it opened up the country; it created fresh wants and stimulated trade with foreign countries. In short, it did many of the things that British rule is believed to be doing at the present day." In spite of this, Wilkinson concluded that "the highly specialised adat Perpateh possesses the greatest possible interest to the study of primitive jurisprudence while the cosmopolitan adat Temenggong is too indefinite and illogical to possess any legal interest whatever" (Hooker, 1970: 38).

Logically, it does not follow that a legal system that has contributed much to the development of society as Wilkinson himself had conceded, should be thus flawed such that it should be of no legal interest at all. Furthermore, if the adat Temenggong did influence the progress of the society as Wilkinson maintained, it is surely not unreasonable to expect a more serious examination of this system of Malay law. Such efforts would certainly allow for a more comprehensive and balanced portrayal of the subject. Yet Wilkinson's writing reveals the contrary.

Attempts at discrediting the adat Temenggong are also at times marred by fallacious reasoning. An instance of such a shortcoming is clearly revealed in Wilkinson's failure to distinguish between bad law and immoral administrators of the law. The adat Temenggong is negatively judged and faulted on the ground that the administrators of the law are despotic and exploitative. In fact, Wilkinson suggested that "despotic administrative authority" is one of the constituent elements of the law, for he clearly stated that "the adat Temenggong was made up of ordinary Malay custom, administered by despotic authority and supplemented by a large number of sumptuary regulations drawn up for the glorification of the court" (page 34).

Though despots may have existed, the law itself, in as far as it does not institutionalize despotic judges and adjudicators, should not be faulted. In fact, Malay laws expressly define the proper conduct of legal administrators. For instance, the Malacca Legal Code (*Undang-Undang Melaka*) stipulates (Liaw, 1976: 71–73) the responsibility of the minister was to, "First, be able to investigate whether a subject is guilty or not, second, to know the law; third, to know how to solve disputes . . . fourth, to hear both parties; fifth to be humane, even at the time of giving severe punishment; and sixth, to know how to conduct an investigation properly."

Probity, fair play and a sense of divine obligation are also demanded of judges as evident in the *Ninety-Nine Laws of Perak*. A provision regulating the duty of judges stipulates that "A judge must ever be mindful of the Almighty and His Prophet; . . . consider the respective positions of himself and his litigants; be on guard against charms and persuasion. After this, he should address himself to the enquiry considering the whole of the evidence." The same legal demands are made of chiefs who are required to

> [b]e just in judgement, for on this depends much good and evil and what is thought good may be found to be the reverse. First the judge must investigate, then make diligent search, then the accused should be confronted with his former misdeeds, then the effects of anger, cajolery and deception should be tried. Then his better feelings should be appealed to. And lastly, he should be severely cross-examined. Lastly we must remember the omnipresence of the Almighty and our office and then only look our enemy in the face. For all men hold a judge as their enemy (Hooker, 1970: 64).

Based on these laws, it would be difficult for an impartial observer to conclude that the adat Temenggong allows for despotic administrators of law. Such an allegation is erroneous in spite of the fact that the real behaviour of those who administer the law may not always coincide with the ethical ideals the law embodies.

Wilkinson's unfavourable evaluation of the adat Temenggong as oppressive is also based on a conscious selection of certain elements found in the laws. Laws that protect the interests of the Malay ruling class are highlighted (Hooker, 1970: 35). Though admittedly, some of these laws were oppressive, they did not make up the entire adat Temenggong. For instance, in the *Undang-Undang Melaka* there are laws which prohibit the common people from using articles of yellow, a privilege reserved only for the members of the Malay ruling class. Likewise, thin and transparent materials are not to be worn on royal grounds. Furthermore, the possession of ornamental sheaths was forbidden and those who possessed gold were not allowed to use them. The rule even extended to children who, except for those of royal parentage, were absolutely prohibited from using gold objects. Then again, only a raja could use a parasol (Liaw, 1976: 63, 69,

173). In the event of a breach of the rules, severe punishment, such as the death sentence, was imposed (page 65). The might and power of the rulers were also reinforced through laws regulating the use of language. Certain words were not to be uttered by ordinary Malay subjects. A subject who uttered them would be put to death (Liaw, 1976: 67). The distinction in the severity of punishment when an individual misappropriated the property of members of the ruling class as opposed to those of the common people also illustrates the point (page 113).

In addition, some of these laws allowed for the exploitation of the Malay masses. As an illustration, the *Undang-Undang Melaka* stipulated that a Malay subject must abide by the commands of the ruler, even if the latter is a tyrannical one (page 67). Furthermore, the Kedah laws also sanctioned forced labour of Malay subjects for the benefit of the ruling class (Winstedt, 1928: 11).[8]

Despite these points, Wilkinson still failed to take into consideration those elements of the adat Temenggong which exhort benevolence on the part of the Malay ruling class for the benefit of their subjects. In the *Ninety-Nine Laws of Perak*, numerous provisions are found which are directed at the rulers to establish social justice and improve the welfare of the Malay masses. Chiefs are demanded by law to consider the welfare of the peasantry (Hooker, 1970: 81). The duties of a village chief (*penghulu*) included ensuring that justice was administered and that cases presented before him were not used for personal gain. The Laws also explicitly states that the ruling class must ensure the creation of "just laws and cheap food" for the good of the people (pages 81–82). As far as the wealthy are concerned, they "must behave with generosity towards the poorer classes. . . . They must give small sums to the devout and make a feast at least once a year without fail and they should earn repute in this world by being charitable to the needy" (page 72).

Even in the *Undang-Undang Melaka*, there are provisions exhorting the ruling class to establish social justice according to injunctions of Islamic law, as laid down in the Quran and the *hadith*. This is clearly revealed in the following article: "Concerning all ministers and the

---

[8] Instances of these adat which institutionalised a wide separation between Malay rulers and the ruled have also been highlighted by Tham Seong Chee (1977: 1–5). The author notes that they entrenched the hierarchical Malay social system and served to maintain the prestige, political power and economic control of the Malay rulers vis-á-viz the commoners.

sida-sida (court officers) and the fighting men, they should act in accordance with the words of God Most High in the Quran; they should obey "the command to do good and the injunction forbidding the doing of evil." The duties of those holding public office were defined as follows: "You should from early morning sit in the hall of audience because God has to a great extent left all human beings to (the care of) the rulers and their ministers, for the Prophet . . . has said . . . all of you, being shepherds, will be questioned about your herds, and therefore, if the occasion arises (we) should willingly take orders and carry out whatever task may be assigned to us in this world so that we may feel without burden in the world to come, because even if the ruler be just, if he has no minister or judges to carry out (his orders) his justice cannot take effect . . ." (Liaw: 163–165). These elements of social justice, namely, concern for the common good and for the forbidding of personal interests of the ruling class to override their duties towards their subjects, found in the adat Temenggong laws, are far from oppressive and unjust. Wilkinson, in failing to take into consideration such laws, reveals the one-sidedness of his claims.

Apart from this shortcoming, Wilkinson also neglected the important contribution of certain elements of the adat Temenggong to the social life of the Malays. Thus, his evaluation is neither comprehensive nor objective. For instance, Wilkinson completely overlooked the immense importance of power conferring laws found in the adat. Hart, in his book the *Concept of Law* defines the objective of such laws as serving to "provide individuals with facilities for realising their wishes, by conferring legal powers upon them to create, by certain specified procedures and subject to certain conditions, structures of rights and duties within the coercive framework of the law." Hart maintains that these laws constitute "one of the greatest contributions of law to social life" (Hart, 1961: 27–28).

The adat Temenggong also comprise innumerable "power conferring rules" fundamental and indispensable to the existence of Malay society. For instance, in the Malay legal digests, we find laws that confer on individuals the power to enter into legal relations with others by marriage, trusteeship, contracts and many other important aspects of social life (Liaw, 127–29; 133–35; 147). Wilkinson, however, evades this significant contribution of the adat Temenggong.

Even the authority of the adat Temenggong as embodied in the legal digests is questioned on the ground that these were not enacted by a legislative authority. To his European audience Wilkinson remarked, "he must not allow himself to be blinded by European preference for written or recorded laws. He should not take the so-called Codes (*Undang-Undang*) too seriously. When he reads about the Malacca Code or the Malay Maritime Code or about the Laws of Bencoolen and Palembang, he has to remember that these so called Codes were never actually enacted by any legislative authority: [t]hey are only digests of Malay laws . . . a digest may give a very faithful picture of its subject but it is, at best a picture and not the actual law . . . they do not possess the authority of enactments. . . ." (Hooker, 1970: 7–8).

Wilkinson's argument that the digests are not enactments may be right, although they may well contain authoritative laws. In English legal history too, authoritative laws that were derived from precedents and customs were embodied in legal digests. These digests carried great weight and their contents were observed throughout the whole kingdom. They were expedient in institutionalizing a common system of law. Though the digests were clearly not the product of legislature, the authority of the laws was certainly acknowledged (Carter, 1907: 59–62). A similar argument could be applied to evaluating the authority of the adat Temenggong. Though the Malay digests were not codes of law enacted by a legislature, this by itself is irrelevant in determining the weight of its authority.[9]

It is pertinent to emphasize that the digests are perhaps the only comprehensive documentary sources of the traditional laws of the Malays. As such, they are significant and cannot be easily disregarded. At the very least, they reflect the spirit of the laws of the

[9] The Malay legal digests date as far back as the fifteenth century. They were believed to have been compiled for the rulers of the Malay States. The compilation of some of these digests spanned over several centuries. The *Undang-Undang Melaka* is a case in point. Several sections of this digest were believed to have dated back to the time of Sultan Muhammad Shah (1424–44) and Sultan Muzaffar Shah (1445–58). The later additions, said to have dated about the beginning of the sixteenth century, were possibly compiled by Sultan Mahmud Shah of Johore (1761–1812). See Liaw, 1976: 38. The *Laws of Kedah*, which contained four different codes, were believed to have been compiled when Sultan Rijaluddin Muhammad Shah ruled at Naga. The oldest of these codes dated 1650 CE (Winstedt, 1928: 1–2). In 1875, an old Minangkabau legal digest from Perak was copied at Penang. According to Winstedt (1953, JMBRAS, Vol XXV1: 1), the digest goes back to c. 1700–28. Yet another digest was compiled for Abd 'l Gafur Mhaiyyudin Shah who ruled Pahang from 1595–1614. It is entitled a Malay Legal Digest (JMBRAS, 1948, Vol. 21, pp. 1–2).

society, even though not all the provisions of the digests may have been enforced. Perhaps it is in this regard that even the colonial writers relied upon them for their appraisal of Malay laws. The works of Crawford, Raffles and Winstedt provide classic instances of this point.

Furthermore, it can in fact be demonstrated that many of the laws and legal principles found in the digests were indeed observed and enforced. Take, for instance, a description of the adat based upon the testimony of Munshi Abdullah's diary, a source Wilkinson himself relied upon in his evaluation of the adat Temenggong. When asked what the laws governing the country were, Abdullah was told: "Don't open your umbrella when passing through the raja's ground, don't wear shoes, don't wear yellow clothes or thin linen. Such things are absolutely illegal." (Hooker, 1970: 34) Clearly, these laws conformed to several provisions of the *Undang-Undang Melaka* (Liaw, 1976: 65–7; 173).

Yet another source utilized by Wilkinson, aspects of which conformed to the Malay legal digests is the *Malay Annals*. A sixteenth century document on the history of the royal house of Malacca, it reveals instances of the similarity between the laws observed with those contained in the Melaka Legal Code. Take, for instance, the rules imposed upon Malay rulers prohibiting them from causing injustice, oppression or cruelty towards their subjects and to administer the masses fairly and efficiently (*Malay Annals*, 1967: 57, 65, 164–65). These clearly conformed to articles 43.2 of the *Undang-Undang Melaka*.

Colonial writers also loved to dwell on the modes of punishment found in the adat Temenggong. Winstedt, for instance, vividly portrayed some of the cruel penalties: "In Malacca, if a great chief were condemned for treason, he was allowed to stab himself or get a relative to do it." Furthermore, the author observed, "these penalties were almost humane compared with the 360 tortures prescribed for traitors in the last section of Abdul al-Ghaffars digest, tortures to be followed by quartering."[10] In addition, Winstedt also mentioned terrible modes of punishment imposed upon commoners. They included taking the offender into the street and "ordering him to be killed or

[10] That 360 tortures will be imposed for treason against the ruler is mentioned in Article 23 of the digest entitled "A Malay Legal Digest" compiled for 'Abd al-Ghafur Muhaiyu'd-din Shah, Sultan of Pahang 1592–1614 AD. It is edited by John E. Kempe and R.O. Winstedt in *JMBRAS*, Vol. XXI, Pt. 1, 1948, p. 40.

impaled or burnt alive or beaten on the chest to death, according to the nature of the crime." Yet another common method of execution in Pahang, according to Winstedt, was to weigh the condemned man's body with a stone and drown him. A variation was to fix the nape of the criminal's neck in a cleft branch and tow him in the wake of a boat till he was dead (Winstedt, 1956: 100–02).

Such modes of punishment, indeed, even worse ones, were also evident in the history of English criminal law particularly after the fifteenth century. Blackstone, the renowned English legal historian, illustrated some of these extremely harsh forms of punishments in his *Commentaries*. For the purpose of comparison, we shall take the example of punishment for treason, which, according to Blackstone "is very solemn and terrible. . . . That the offender be drawn to the gallows, and not be carried or walked, though usually a sledge or hurdle is allowed to preserve the offender from the extreme torment of being dragged on the ground or pavement; that he be hanged by the neck, and then cut down alive; that his entrails be taken out, and burned, while he is yet alive; that his head be cut off; that his body be divided into four parts; that his head and quarters be at the king's disposal." Furthermore, the author noted that almost the same form of punishment was applied to women (Blackstone, 1966: 92–3). Brutal methods of execution were common. As one author observed:

> the most morbid imagination today can hardly picture the variety of tortures inflicted . . . executions by knives, axe and sword, heads being sawed off with a plank or cut through a plough, people being buried alive, left to stay in a dungeon, or having nails hammered through heads, eyes, shoulders and knees, strangulation, throttling, drowning, bleeding to death, evisceration, drowning and quartering, tortures on the wheel, tortures with red-hot tongs, strips being cut away from the skin, body being torn to pieces or sawed through with iron or wooden instruments, burning at the stake and many other violent acts of cruelty. It is not surprising that practically every crime was punishable by death and that the vital question was the manner in which death should be inflicted (Rusche and Kircheimer, 1939: 21–2).

Not only were these forms of punishment extremely harsh and cruel, they were also imposed on a large number of people. The data on England in the course of the sixteenth century reveals the immense extent of these tortures. Seventy-two thousand minor and major thieves were hanged during the reign of Henry VIII, and under

Elizabeth, vagabonds were strung up in rows as many as three and four hundred at a time. The population of England then was only about three million (page 19).[11] By contrast, although Malay society also experienced brutal modes of punishment, these were never imposed on Malay subjects on such a massive scale.

Problems of definition also abound in these writings. Wilkinson, for instance, failed to draw a conceptual distinction between adat law and adat as the totality of customs practiced in Malay society. The failure to distinguish these forms of social control is evident in his attempts at comparing adat with English law, as the following passage illustrates:

> Adat is right procedure. In all matters there is a right way of doing things and a wrong way of doing things; adat is the right way..In English, the word 'law' is used in a loose popular sense as well as in a technical sense; adat is law in the loose popular sense. Adat includes the laws of nature, the conventions of society, the rules of etiquette and even the doctrines of common sense. Adat is right action in matters of everyday life as well as obedience to the law of the land. The English word 'law' as defined by a great jurist like Austin, is adat in a very limited sense indeed, it does not cover the so-called laws of nature or of health or of etiquette (Hooker, 1970: 15).

Though it has been generally recognized that, in some instances, law being part of social rules, may not be sharply separable from it, nevertheless, legal scholars have acknowledged the need to draw this conceptual distinction in the vast majority of cases. As Van Vollenhoven aptly remarks, "But this overlapping of custom and customary law need not prevent a separation between the two because in many instances, it is easy to distinguish the adat with legal consequences and to set them apart from the adat without legal consequences" (Van Vollenhoven, 1981: 6). Even in English legal history, courts make a clear distinction between customs and law despite the fact that in some cases a clear distinction between the two forms of social control may be difficult to draw.[12]

Having failed to draw a conceptual distinction between adat law and other social rules, Wilkinson (Hooker, 1970: 15) implied that

---

[11] A description of the severity of judicial sentiments on retribution in the late Middle Ages is also highlighted by Huizinga (1924: 11, 12, 22–24).

[12] For a further discussion on the relation between law and custom in English legal history, please see Sadler (1919, chapter 4); see also MacIver (1937: 358–63).

traditional Malays are not enlightened enough to make this distinction. Such an implication can be deduced from his following remark,

> Curiously enough, the modern Minangkabau Malays have been clear-sighted enough to appreciate the difference between law and adat as the following verse will prove: Orang Mekkah membawa teraju, Orang Baghdad membawa telor, Dimakan dalam puasa. Rumah yang bersendi batu, Adat yang bersendi *law* [italics mine], Itu-lah akan raja.

Wilkinson's argument, however, is erroneous due to inaccuracies in translation. The key word, "law" in the stanza above has been erroneously translated from the original Malay word '*halur*' that in fact means, customarily observed.[13] As such, the stanza cannot be used to support his claim that until recently, Malays are not clear-sighted enough to appreciate a distinction between law and adat. On the contrary, it is Wilkinson himself who failed to perceive such a distinction.

In a way, Wilkinson's argument that until recently Malays made no distinction between adat law and other social norms revealed shortcomings similar to those found in the conceptions of certain anthropologists on primitive law, such as those of Hartland, Driberg, Meek and others. The authors, in considering the nature of law in non-Western societies, have asserted that law, as a distinct phenomenon, did not exist. These views have been severely criticised by Hoebel (1954: 20–21) in his book "The Law of Primitive Man" as the conceptions of a "lawless anthropology."

The conceptualization and evaluation of Malay adat laws by colonial writers reveal serious misperceptions, an ethnocentric bias, and the negative influence of ideology. These shortcomings created a distorted image of the adat law, one that is neither accurate nor objective.

---

[13] The complete article is as follows:
Bring the jackfruit to the pot
To be cooked during the fast
What is the duty of the official?
To obey the ruler's orders
And if the country has no rulers, then abide by the Tradition of the Malays:
The people of Mecca bring their scales
Those from Medinah bring along eggs
To be eaten during the month of fast
Like a firm house built on stone,
Adat which are customarily observed
Will be honoured as our ruler.

CHAPTER THREE

ISLAM AND ITS RELATIONSHIP WITH MALAY ADAT LAWS

Perceptions of the influence of Islam on Malay adat laws abound in the writings of Raffles, Wilkinson, Winstedt and Hooker. In many respects, their views and judgments reveal serious problems in conceptualization so that a discussion of this issue is pertinent. Significant shortcomings stem mainly from scanty knowledge of Islam as well as of Malay adat laws. These severely affect their understanding of Islam and its relationship with the adat. The authors also failed to grasp accurately the extent of the influence of Islam on Malay adat laws. Furthermore, many of the arguments are marred by misconceptions and bias against Islam as revealed in the portrayal of the effects of Islam on adat laws. In this chapter, attempts will be made to portray these inadequacies and to show how they obstruct an objective representation of Islam as an element that has influenced Malay adat laws.

A clear manifestation of these shortcomings is revealed in the misleading and over-generalized portrayal of the relationship between Islam and Malay adat laws. For example, Raffles, as we have earlier shown, subscribed to the view that Islam being "radically different" from local customary laws, failed to harmonize effectively with it. Raffles (1935: 98), however, provided no concrete examples to substantiate his claim.

The argument that Islam did not synthesize with the adat laws finds support in the writings of Wilkinson. According to Wilkinson (Hooker, 1970: 6), the adat "did not harmonize with the doctrine of Islam they professed to follow." Moreover, they were conceived to be "absolutely irreconcilable" and could not be more unlike one another. Like Raffles, Wilkinson provided no concrete illustrations in support of his claim.

Such a perception is misleading. It portrays a one-sided and static conception of both Islam and the adat law, which is unjustified not only in the light of Islamic legal history and precepts but also on the evidence provided by the Malay legal digests.[1] Theoretically, Islam accommodates customary laws so long as these are in consonance with its essential doctrine and principles. This is supported by some of the following sayings of the Prophet Muhammed (*ahadith*), which constitutes one of the chief sources of Islamic law. For example, one Prophetic saying states that "[t]he virtues of the days of ignorance (*jahiliyyah*) will be acted upon in Islam."; another says that "a wise counsel is the lost property of the faithful (*Mu'min*); whenever he discovers it, he takes hold of it" (Shariff, 1966: 1229).[2] Though couched in general terms, these *hadith* are relevant to illustrating that Islam assimilates and does not reject customary laws and practices that are consistent with its teachings. Even the stipulation in the Quran that "all that is not expressly forbidden is lawful" renders support to this principle (Quran 4: 24).[3]

In addition, in its historical and empirical manifestations, Islam had, from its inception, accommodated and allowed for the continued observance of many local customary laws which were in harmony with its teachings. For instance, Islam incorporated and modified a large part of the system of virtues regulated by traditional legal ideas of the Saracens. These included the rendering of protection to those who sought aid; the observance of duties connected with family ties (Goldziher, 1967; vol. 1: 22–23), nomadic virtues of generosity (Watt, 1953: 74–75), the principle of arbitration in the settlement of disputes (Schacht, 1964: 7–8) and many others. Islam also incorporated many legal customs of other civilizations that were brought under its sovereignty. For instance, it retained the pre-Islamic Sassanian system of the law of land revenue after Caliph Umar found

[1] That there existed elements of adat laws inconsistent with Islam is undeniable. It is, however, beyond the scope of this limited study to determine precisely how much of the adat is inconsistent with Islam, although illustrations of inconsistencies are highlighted where necessary. The overriding objective of this chapter is to show that, contrary to the views of adat law writers, Islam has the capacity to accommodate and assimilate those adat which are in consonance with its doctrine. For an interesting discussion on the problem of conflict between adat and Islam, please refer to Othman Ishak, *Hubungan antara Undang-Undang Islam dan Undang-Undang Adat*, Dewan Bahasa dan Pustaka, K.L., 1979.

[2] These *hadith* are related on the authority of Ibn Hanbal and al-Tirmidhi respectively. For further references, please see M. Hamidullah (Sharif, 1966: Vol. 2, 1229).

[3] A.Y. Ali, *The Holy Quran: Text, Translation and Commentary*, Publications of Presidency of Islamic Courts and Affairs State of Qatar, 1946, IV, 24. A discussion of this principle of Islamic law is highlighted by Syekh Yusuf Qardhawi (1980: 14–19).

such a system equitable and in conformity with social justice (Sharif, 1966: Vol. 2, 1230).[4] The effect of the influence of Islam on Malay adat laws is no different.

One of the most significant and enlightening evidence of the relationship between Islam and Malay adat laws is found in Article 71 of the *Undang-Undang Sungei Ujong*. The provision not only reveals that Malay adat law and Islam can be reconciled, it also explains the basis of this integration. The article (Winstedt and de Jong, 1954: 51–52) reads as follows:

> adat confirms religious law as is said in the *hadith* ". . . when adat has a strong position in a country, it serves as religious law", for the strength of adat is based on the consensus of all religious scholars and the Companions of the Prophet. For that reason, adat is strengthened, religious law is enforced, both are employed to the present day, unchanging down the generations, handed from our ancestors.

The harmonious relationship between adat law and Islam is also expressed in the adat of Jelebu as follows:

> Adat hinges on religious law,
> Religious law hinges on the Book of God.
> If adat is strong, religious law does not oppose it,
> If religious law is strong, adat does not oppose it.
> The source of religious law is consensus,
> The source of adat is consensus (Caldecott, 1918: 26).[5]

It is pertinent to rectify indications of misconceptions by authors such as Wilkinson that these propositions cannot be considered accurate representations of the harmonious relationship between Islam and Malay adat laws. For instance, Wilkinson (Hooker, 1970: 7) notes that the Malays "pretend indeed to regard the adat as explanatory of Muslim law or as supplementary to it." According to him, "all this is mere fiction, the three legal systems are absolutely irreconcilable." Quoting relevant provisions from the digests on the conciliatory relationship between Islam and the adat, Wilkinson (Hooker,

[4] For a more detailed account of the process and instances of assilimilation, modification and rejection of pre-Islamic customary laws of the Arabs during the early period of development of Islamic jurisprudence, please refer to J. Schacht's discussion in "Pre Islamic Background and Early Development of Jurisprudence" in *Law in the Middle East*. Vol. 1 (ed.), M. Khadduri, Middle East Institute, Washington, 1955.

[5] Some insights into the relationship between Islam and Malay culture can also be found in S.H. Alatas (1979: 38–48).

1970: 20–21) explains away their significance by asserting that "... the Negri Sembilan Malay affects to believe that Moslem law agrees with the adat ..." Yet Wilkinson did not provide grounds for this impression. As such, it is not unreasonable to judge his claims as biased generalizations. Wilkinson ignored the fact that these provisions are authoritative ideal expressions of Malay laws. In the Peninsula, where the Malays are Muslims, the ideal of the law is one based on Islamic values and teachings with the support of adat consistent with Islamic precepts. As such, these provisions clearly state the sources of authority of Malay laws and the harmonious and supportive nature of their relationship.

As ideal statements of the adat, they are not absolute facts. They may not conform wholly to the existing laws of the society. Nevertheless, they are not mere "fiction" as Wilkinson asserts. Nor can these ideal statements be perceived as indications of pretension on the part of the Malays. The acknowledgement of the ideal element in law which may be inconsistent with existing law does not logically reveal a pretentious attitude. In this respect, the argument of the renowned jurist Roscoe Pound on the significance of the ideal element in Western legal thought may perhaps illustrate our point. Pound pointed out that the ideal elements in Western law based either on the doctrines of Christianity or natural law or that of laissez faire which find their way into legal codes do not always accord precisely with existing laws. Nevertheless, he argues, to show that such ideals are not wholly realized in practice in no way disposes of them, for they are much a part of the authoritative legal materials by which justice is administered. Furthermore, they also serve as authoritative starting points for legal reasoning and provide principles by which laws are selected, interpreted and applied (Pound, 1958: chapter 1). In much the same way, it can be argued that Islamic elements in adat laws, which may not accord totally with existing laws, are nevertheless significant as authoritative sources of the law. They provide the criteria, acknowledged by the society, upon which adat laws are justified, applied and interpreted. The very fact that there is a need to justify the adat as consistent with Islam reveals the importance attached to this ideal element.

The Malay legal digests also bear revealing evidence of harmony between Islam and adat laws. There is, for instance, no inconsistency between them on matters which pertain to the fundamental aspects of social life. The *Undang-Undang Melaka*, for instance clearly reveals that Islam accommodates and strengthens adat laws in fundamental matters such as those pertaining to violations of person and property. These include murder, theft, slashing, slaying, abusing people, rape and many others (Liaw, 1976: 69, 71, 75, 77, 83, 85). Although this digest reveals that Islam prescribes a different form of punishment for some of these offences, yet essentially, Islam, like adat law, explicitly recognizes the respect for life, honour and property necessary for the preservation of social life. Though this is an extremely important piece of evidence on the harmonious relationship between Islam and Malay adat laws, none of the writers, in their enthusiasm to portray the incapacity of Islam to synthesize with adat, took this into consideration.

That their evaluation is an over generalized one is also supported by the fact that in many instances the writers' knowledge of pre-Islamic customary laws, which constitutes one of the essential elements for evaluation, is limited.[6] In the *Undang-Undang Melaka*, for instance, several essential aspects reflect strong Islamic influence. (Ibrahim and Joned, 1986: 46–7) Some of these pertain to the realm of family law, to laws regulating transactions and procedural justice (Liaw, 1976: 27–37, 151–53). These serve to show that the adat has harmoniously assimilated many aspects of Islam so that it is misleading to highlight conflicts in the relationship between Islam and Malay adat laws.

The view that Islam is irreconcilable with adat laws also finds support in the writings of Hooker. He attempted to explain the source of this conflict by arguing that Islam is inherently irreconcilable with the adat because of the revealed nature of Islamic law and the foreign content of the *hadith*. Thus, he asserts (Hooker, 1984: 3–4):

> It must never be forgotten that Islam is a religion (and a law) of the book: Kitab. This is not merely a statement about Revelation but a reference to the source of knowledge. While Revelation incorporates its own system of obligation, this system may or may not fit easily or combine with non-revelationary realities, whether economic, social, political or legal. Islam is thus characteristically, an ethos of tension resulting from the existence of multiple sets of obligations coexisting within a single culture. It is this last which has major consequences for Southeast Asian Islamic law. The great majority of the Muslims of this area are of the Shafie school. Following the doctrine of their

[6] The issue of sources of preIslamic adat is also touched upon by Taufik Abdullah (1966, Vol. 2: 9–10).

> founder and their subsequent scholarly elaboration, the version of Islamic jurisprudence to which they were exposed laid primacy on the Sunna as the definition of Quran. However, the Hadith, the vehicle of the Sunna, which describes the practice or opinion or custom in question was itself cast in unfamiliar and foreign terms. For the Malays . . . the Middle Eastern hadith do not represent local or regional cultural elements. The result is not that the people of the area were less Muslim than their co-religionists elsewhere but that a state of tension between Islamic principles and local culture is the characteristic feature of the area. It manifests itself in different ways and nowhere is this more clearly apparent than in Muslim literature.

It is evident that, for Hooker, one of the chief sources of incompatibility between Islam and adat laws lies in the revealed source of Islamic law. Such a view is misleading. Although Islamic law is divine in origin, yet it is human in its subject matter and oriented towards the practical needs of society. Thus, according to de Santillana (1949: 290), in Islam "Positive law (shariah, the straight way) is the discipline of human activity as directed to earthly purposes." A noted Muslim jurist also asserts that the law essentially serves the needs of men by removing hardship and not for the glorification of the Lawgiver (Abdur Rahim, 1963: 43). Incompatibility is not therefore a consequence of the revelationary nature of Islamic law as opposed to non-revelationary ones but in the substance propagated by the laws which seek to regulate equally human concerns to attain specific ends. In the case of Islam, the end or purpose of law is the conscious attainment of the well being of man (de Santillana, 1949: 290). The sole principle that guides legislative activity in all cases is "to do what is good, and abstain from doing what is evil" (Hamidullah, 1966: 1221–23).

According to Hooker, the other source of incompatibility between Islam and Malay laws lies in the *hadith* which he believed to be culturally specific and hence alien to the Malays. This perception is erroneous and reveals Hooker's scant knowledge of Islam. The assertion negates innumerable *hadith* which embody universal values, valid cross-culturally. For instance, the Prophet Muhammad's commands that men should help those in distress, that they should not hurt animals, that they should keep their promises, respect the proprietary rights of others, speak the truth, judge justly, not cause harm or destruction to people, respect life, avoid oppression and injustice, are but some of the innumerable universal precepts applicable to any society (Ameer Ali, 1946: 137–158 and Shariff, 1966: 165–177).

Hooker's conception of the *hadith* as foreign to the Malays reveals yet another significant shortcoming. He fails to draw a conceptual distinction between the culturally specific and the universal contents of the *hadith*.[7] Although some of them are woven into specifically Arabian or Middle Eastern practice, nevertheless, the Malays generally distinguish the Islamic elements from the specific cultural context of these provisions. For instance, it has been narrated on the authority of Abu Dharr that the Prophet had remarked that among those whom God would not absolve on the day of resurrection is the dragger of the lower garment (Muslim, 1977: Vol. 1, 60–61). This *hadith* condemns as improper the manner of use of a form of attire alien to the Malays. However, most Malays are aware that the relevance of the *hadith* lies not in its culturally specific example but in the more fundamental ethical principle, namely, the admonishment against pride. It was regarded as a sign of arrogance in Arabian society during that era to drag one's lower garment.

Yet another example revealing the error of Hooker's reasoning is found in a *hadith* recorded by Abu Hurairah, in which the Prophet was said to have prohibited the townsmen to sell to a man from the desert (Muslim, Vol. 3, 800–801). Contextually, the conditions portrayed in the *hadith* are inapplicable to Malay conditions. However, the more universal meaning of this *hadith* as understood by most Malays is that brokerage is unlawful if it is carried out with a view to taking advantage of the client's ignorance of market conditions.

Apart from portraying the view that Islam is irreconcilable with the adat, the writers also sought to show that the influence of Islam on Malay laws results in negative consequences. Raffles, for instance, believed that the inability of Islam to synthesize with the original laws of the Malays created diversification in the realm of law. This resulted in a complex and ill-defined system of law governing essential aspects of social life, which in turn paved the way for capricious rule and a general insecurity of person and property (Raffles, 1835: 99).

Raffles' argument that Islam is the cause of diversification in law is erroneous. He fails to take into consideration the fact that prior to the coming of Islam, the Malays were already exposed to other

[7] The need to distinguish between these two factors in understanding Islam has been pointed out by S.H. Alatas (1956: 8).

influences that had affected the unification of laws. Before the advent of Islam, the Malay World was already diversified based on ethnic, linguistic, political and religious lines. In fact, historically, Islam contributed to bringing about political and legal unification in Java, Sumatra and the Malay Peninsula. Thus, according to Alatas "historically and sociologically, Raffles' view on the causes of diversification is unsound. Diversification was there long before the coming of Islam." In fact according to Alatas, it was Islam that first introduced a common system of law (1977: 130–31).

In any case, it does not logically follow that diversification led to tyranny and created an insecurity of person and property. On the contrary, the coming of Islam circumscribed the powers of the Malay ruling class and defined their rights and obligations towards their subjects in no uncertain terms. These rules of law are clearly stipulated in written legal digests after the coming of Islam.[8]

For instance, the articles in the *Undang-Undang Melaka* make statements to the effect that rulers are to rule justly, and this is explicitly influenced by Islam (Liaw, 1976: 163–65). Justice, benevolence and patience are also enjoined upon rulers and chiefs in dealing with their subjects. Articles 13 and 19 of the *Minangkabau Digest from Perak* also corroborate this fact unlike Raffles' assertion that Islam brought about the rule of tyranny (Winstedt, 1953: 4).

Yet another erroneous conjecture expounded by Raffles is the notion that diversification in laws caused by Islam brought about insecurity of person and property. Raffles overlooked the fact Islam strengthened and accommodated fundamental rules of law respecting the life and property of the Malays. In the *Undang-Undang Melaka* laws stipulating the conditions for valid contractual agreements, regulations against usurpation of trusts, prohibitions against usury, and many other laws regulating the protection of life and property, bear the unmistakable influence of Islam.

For example, Islam emphasizes that any contractual agreement, including that of a trust, be reduced to writing in the presence of at least two witnesses. This is formally enjoined in the Quran in (11: 282). It stipulates the following:

> ... when ye deal with each other, in transactions involving future obligations in a fixed period of time, reduce them to writing ... And get

[8] For further discussions, please refer to Chapter 5.

> two witnesses out of your own men, and if there are not two men, then a man and two women, such as ye choose for witnesses, so that if one of them errs, the other can remind her.

The following verse 283 also commands trustees to discharge their trusts faithfully and not to misappropriate trust property knowingly: ". . . And if one of you deposits a thing on trust with another, let the trustee (faithfully) discharge his trust . . ." These conditions are clearly reflected in the *Undang-Undang Melaka* which states that: "when a man deposits a trust . . . it should be done in the presence of witnesses and accompanied by a written document." Furthermore, the spirit of the Quranic injunction pertaining to the obligations of the trustee is also reflected in this legal digest as follows:

> If the trustee accepts the trust, he should keep it in the same place where he keeps his own property . . . If the trustee makes use of the trust even if it is with the consent of the owner . . . and it gets lost, the trustee has to pay compensation. When the trustee wishes to sail, the trust should be returned to the owner; if the owner is not present, it should be returned to his agent or to the judge or to the imam (religious leader) . . . (Liaw, 1976: 147).

That the laws on contracts in the *Undang-Undang Melaka* also reveal the influence of Islam is reflected in the conditions regulating a sale. According to Islam, one of the factors invalidating the contract is the issue of incapacity. Among the chief causes of incapacity are drunkenness, lunacy, slavery or that the party to the agreement is a minor (Kadduri, 1955: 196–98). These are clearly reflected in the *Undang-Undang Melaka* as follows:

> With regards to laws pertaining to sale, it is not valid to trade unless with someone who is sane, . . . and it is also invalid to trade with a child who is yet of age and furthermore, it is invalid to trade with a person who is intoxicated . . . because such a person who is intoxicated with alcohol is not certain of the price of the article which he offers for sale or about the article itself. Furthermore, that it is invalid to trade with someone else's slave unless the latter has got permission from his master to trade (Liaw, 1976: 135).

Islam also regulates the validity of the object of transaction. For instance, the object traded must be capable of delivery, permissible in law, specific, sufficiently known to the contracting parties and, finally, it must be in existence (Kadduri, 1955: 194). These conditions are again reflected in the *Undang-Undang Melaka* revealing a strong Islamic influence. Article 30 stipulates: "The article for sale should be pure and it is invalid to trade in impure things such as alcoholic drinks and dogs and pigs and other forbidden things. It is valid to trade in things which are useful . . . the sale is valid if the seller is able to deliver the article . . . an article that is available for inspection should be inspected, the article described should exactly match the description given by the seller . . .". Even the prohibition against usury for those who trade is again Islamic (Liaw: 135). The Quran itself clearly states that: ". . . God hath permitted trade and forbidden usury" (Quran 11: 275).

Unfavourable influence of Islam is further highlighted by Wilkinson who asserts that Islam "multiplies offences intolerably." Among the offences for which Wilkinson (Hooker, 1970: 9–10) views as harsh are cockfighting, opium smoking and gambling. He fails to admit that these are acts that do not promote the welfare of the individual, and that many societies regard the consumption of opium as an offence, while gambling, though legally sanctioned in some, has never received universal social approval. To some extent, Wilkinson's view may have been ideologically motivated. Opium and gambling were among the two sources of business from which the British derived substantial revenue. The licence and sale of their monopolies raked in large profits that benefitted the colonial power (Alatas, 1977: 91, 206). As such, laws prohibiting the Malays from partaking in these activities would undermine any potential profit accruing to the colonial power.

Yet another instance whereby the influence of Islam is perceived negatively is evident in the writings of Hooker, who subscribed to the view that Islam creates tension in society (Hooker, 1984: 36) This was allegedly brought about by the conflict between Islam and some aspects of adat law. This argument is rather simplistic, as it presumes the absence of conflicts within the traditional adat order prior to the coming of Islam. On the contrary, it has been argued that the few sources of pre-Islamic adat of Minangkabau society reveal that internal conflicts between the ideal of adat and its local variations and realities had indeed existed, as did efforts at reconciliation. In fact, such conflicts were recognized within the society even before Islam influenced the adat (Taufik Abdullah, 1966: Vol. 2, 3–13).

Furthermore, Hooker did not evaluate the effects of such tension He did not distinguish between the positive and negative effects of tension in concrete terms. To my mind, such a distinction is crucial in judging its consequences on society. For instance, many of the laws introduced into Arabian society at the inception of Islam were alien and opposed to the prevailing customary laws of the Arabs. The introduction of these new regulations created tension in the society. Prohibitions against usury, the excesses of blood feud, hoarding, burning of daughters alive, consumption of intoxicating drinks, abuse of slaves, possession of widows by their step-sons, gambling and prostitution, were some of the numerous rules which severely conflicted with the approved practices of the time.[9] Yet it cannot be denied that these profound innovations introduced by Islam improved the condition of the society.

Wilkinson (Hooker, 1970: 32) also blamed Islam for corrupting the originally "humane", "simple" and "democratic" adat Perpateh of the Malays. It was through the influence of Islam that the "autocratic", "inhumane" adat Temenggong evolved. Wilkinson implies therefore that the influence of Islam on the adat Perpateh is minimal if at all.

Winstedt (1953: 98–99) extends this view even further by suggesting that the adat Perpateh was not strongly influenced by Islam. The following utterances convey this notion:

> put its customary provisions alongside the despotic and brutal hybrid law of the patriarchal Malay States and at once it is apparent why this matrilineal law commands the passionate regard of the Minangkabau as a Magna Carta . . . No Raja ever dared to tamper with its validity and no Muslim Kathi to challenge its unorthodox principles. It was safe in the keeping of democracy of inland agriculturalists impervious to foreign influence.

The notion that the adat Perpateh is not strongly influenced by Islam, as suggested by Winstedt and, to some extent, Wilkinson, is baseless. In fact, the very adat Perpateh that they speak of is saturated with fundamental teachings of Islam. The failure of the authors to take into account glaring evidence of such influence reveals a lack of thoroughness and accuracy of their claims. Attempts at explaining away or denying the influence of Islam on the adat Perpateh which the authors conceive as a sound legal system reveal a strong

[9] For an account of some of these preIslamic customs and the effects of the influence of Islam on the society, please refer to Syed Amir Ali, *The Spirit of Islam*, op. cit., M. Watt, Mohammad at Mecca, op. cit., and S.H. Alatas, *Democracy of Islam*, op. cit.

bias against Islam. The refusal to associate Islam with the adat Perpateh is but part of the wider and consistent attempts at undermining the positive influences of Islam on Malay laws. We will attempt to show the distortion by pointing out several significant instances of the unmistakable influence of Islam on the adat Perpateh.

One of the most fundamental manifestations of the influence of Islam on the adat Perpateh lies in the fact that Islam is explicitly recognized as an essential source of the adat. This is evident in the *perbilangan* of Jelebu which stipulates Quranic law as one of the authoritative sources of adat (Caldecott, 1918: 10, 26). The adherence to Islamic sources of law is also expressed in the *Undang-Undang Sungei Ujong*. Article 4 stipulates that "Truth arises out of three things, out of consensus, Allah's Book and Ancestral lore." Furthermore, the sources of Truth are recognized to be "the word of Allah, the reasoning and traditions of Allah's messenger, the decisions of the divines and the religious leaders Shafie, Hanafi, Hanbali and Maliki, and Allah's Prophet Adam, on whom be peace" (Winstedt and de Jong, 1954: 40). In stipulating the six sources of the adat, the digest makes constant reference to Islam. They are:

1. ancient custom (*cupak yang asli*)
2. created custom (*cupak buatan*)
3. inherited tradition (*kata pusaka*)
4. decisions of common accord (*kata muafakat*)
5. ancient custom that awaits ratification (*kata dahulu yang ditepati*)
6. decisions to be reached by later deliberation (*kata kemudian kata bercari*) (pages 40–41).

Ancient custom which embodies principles of justice and which is regarded as absolute reveals its Islamic influence as follows: "That is the custom followed by the inhabitants of Mekka and Medina, of Acheh . . . and which then reached us." The Islamic element of this source of law is further reinforced by a quotation from the Quranic verse exhorting justice: "When ye judge among men, judge with righteousness" (page 41).

"Created custom" is defined as custom that comes from the findings of intelligent chiefs or of the people of the country, village or clan. It may agree with religious law or contravene it, and it is affirmed in each district or clan by the recital of the creed of Islam, sprinkling rice paste, slaughtering a buffalo, and so forth (page 42). The provision has been completely misconstrued by writers such as Hooker, who are quick to define this source of adat as unIslamic. Hooker asserts that "there appears to be a purely Malay influence as opposed to Islamic or Hindu affectations" in this provision. According to Hooker, "created custom, may contravene canon, i.e., Islamic law, if the provisions of the former are introduced with due ceremony, for instance, by the sprinkling of rice paste or the slaughtering of buffaloes, neither ceremony being Koranic" (Hooker, 1968: 159–60).

Neither the sprit nor the content of this provision is consistent with Hooker's interpretation. It is inconceivable for Hooker to suggest that "created custom" which contravenes the Sharia is also recognized as valid law. The numerous provisions in the digest that attribute immense importance to Islam render such an interpretation fallacious and inconsistent. The actual meaning of the article is that, because created custom lacks the certainty of revealed law, it may, as a matter of fact, contravene religious law. This explains why in creating it the recitation of the opening verse of the Quran, "*al-Fatihah*", or the creed of Islam is observed. Such an act implies the hope that the law created is one that is in accordance with the doctrines of Islam. Associated customary practices such as the sprinkling of ricc paste and the slaughtering of buffaloes are neutral to the injunctions of Islam, which neither prohibits nor encourages these practices. Thus, contrary to Hooker's allegation, nothing in the provision can be said to be inconsistent with Islam. The provision also reveals that the influence of Islam on Malay adat laws is so pervasive that to speak of "Malay" as opposed to "Islamic affectations" as Hooker had done is misleading and distorts an accurate representation of these laws. The other sources of law stipulated above which require the use of reason do not contradict Islamic legal principles. In the history of Islamic law innumerable precepts were multiplied and new laws introduced by the successors of the Prophet Muhammad, which were deemed necessary to meet the changing conditions of society (Ameer Ali, 1899: 55–69).

Apart from the sources of law, the influence of Islam on the adat is also evident in matters pertaining to procedural justice. A pertinent case in point is found in the prescribed rules governing arbitrators of law and those involved in litigation. In Islam, moral conduct such as regularity, impartiality and righteousness are strictly demanded of those involved in litigation. Violation of the principle of the mean is severely condemned. Thus the Quran bids one to arbitrate with justice and not to deviate from the truth while judging between men

(Quran, IV: 58–9). In addition, those involved in litigation must also have the ability to conduct investigations impartially and possess knowledge of the law to solve disputes in a prudent and objective manner.[10]

These principles are reflected in the provisions of the digest. A judge's duties, according to the *Undang-Undang Sungei Ujong*, are eight:

1. to examine witnesses
2. to make decisions
3. to bring opposing parties together
4. to fear Allah Most High
5. to keep circumstantial evidence
6. to order punishment
7. to judge with equity according to Allah's commands . . . (Winstedt and de Jong, 1954: 53–4)

(The eighth duty is omitted due to lack of clarity and incompleteness of the relevant provision.) Of all the types of counsellors, the Digest credits the "kinglike" counsellor with the highest merit. Consistent with Islamic conceptions,

> they are active both morning and night and are sorry when they observe people to be at enmity and daily weigh the cause of disputes without thinking it a trouble . . . If he is contradicted by a litigant and accused of mis-statements, then he turns to the other party and replies: We are overcome. Now we shall think it over a whole day. Once we have thought of something good, we shall oppose again (page 53).

Even substantive justice embodied in the adat Perpateh is Islamic. Take, for instance, Article 17, categorized as "Laws of the Country." It reads thus:

> Whoever wounds must pay a fine, whoever kills must replace blood money, who wrongly eats must spit out, who wrongly seizes must restore, who goes astray must return, who sins against God, must repent, who offends unintentionally pays the fine (or asks pardon), lies are rejected, impartial inquiry is employed, when an account is correct, one pays; when it is wrong, one disputes, one must do it in public. The joint earnings of man and wife are divided; who seizes must restore, the borrower returns, debts are paid, what it is owed is received. If the debtor is afar, he can be pursued, if near there can be distraint of his goods (pages 45–46).

[10] For a further discussion on the qualifications and duties of judges please see Ali Ibn Abi Talib's *Nahjul Balagha* (Jafri, 1984: 634).

The punishments described for the offences above are consistent with the options allowed by Islam, which enjoins the payment of compensation by an offender to a victim or his family for having committed physical injury or murder. Such a mode of punishment, which is acknowledged by Islam as an alternative to incarceration, is specifically stipulated in SV verse 48 of the Quran, as follows: "We ordained therein for them, life for life, tooth for tooth and wounds equal for equal. But if anyone remits the retaliation by way of charity, it is an act of atonement for himself."

Furthermore, Islamic influence is also reflected in the adat law that allows for anyone who wrongfully seizes or appropriates the property of another to restore the same. If it has been consumed, destroyed or lost, he must replace it if it is replaceable property (Kadduri, 1955: 189). As far as borrowing is concerned, Islam makes it obligatory that the debt must be duly paid to the creditor even after death. In the event that the debtor is insolvent, he may be declared bankrupt and his property sold so that the proceeds can be distributed to his creditors (Al-Nawawi, 1914: 162). Furthermore, consistent with the adat, Islam promotes the principle that joint earnings of husband and wife are to be equally divided, for the Quran stipulates that "to men is allotted what they earn, and to women what they earn" (S1V, Verse 32).

The adat procedure to be observed in the settlement of disputes also bears a close similarity to the teachings of Islam, which state that a judge must be impartial and must be able to sieve through evidence from lies. Where the defendant is capable of being sued, the action takes place in public. If the defendant denies the charge, the plaintiff produces his evidence; if he cannot do so if witnesses are absent, the defendant is asked to take an oath whereby God Almighty is invoked as his witness, and that he incurs the wrath of God upon himself should he be telling a lie (Schacht, 1964: 188–90).

Islam also provides the ethical basis for numerous provisions of the adat Perpateh. What are deemed as "evil customs" by the adat are similarly scorned by Islam. These include gambling, destruction of another's property, causing harm and hurt to others, deceiving others and many other destructive and harmful acts (Winstedt and de Jong, 1954: 62).[11] In some instances, the authority of Islam is

[11] That Islam scorns gambling is evident in S 11, verse 219 of the Quran. Islam also admonishes those who hurt or deceive others. See the Quran S V Verse 3 and S IX Verse 119 respectively.

explicitly invoked. Thus, in condemning the oppression and injustice of those who rule, recourse is made to relevant *hadith* for the case in point (page 62). In the light of these examples that portray a decisive influence of Islam, the assertion of the writers that the adat Perpateh is impervious to foreign influence, namely Islam, is completely baseless.

The writers' negative assessment of the influence of Islam on Malay adat laws and their attempts at convincing their audience that Islam did not strongly influence the adat Perpateh despite substantial evidence to the contrary, may have been conditioned by a deeply rooted ideological bias against Islam. It is here reiterated that, by ideology, we mean a system of beliefs characterizing the interests of a distinctive group which seeks to justify a particular social and economic order. In so doing, it distorts that part of social reality likely to contradict its main presuppositions (Alatas, 1977: 1). By propagating the view that Islamic influence on the adat is minimal and negative, the writers justify their attempts at checking the further and gradual influence of Islamic forces and ideas on the evolution of Malay adat laws.

The function of such ideas can only be adequately understood in the context of contending interests, dating back to as early as the sixteenth century, between Western imperialism and the Muslims in the Malay Archipelago. Islam served as the rallying point against the onslaught of the Portuguese (Schrieke, 1955: 37–48). Dutch involvement also met with severe opposition and resistance crystallized around Islam. A well known uprising which revealed the potent political threat of Islam was the Acheh war which dragged on for many years. Islam was also the basis of the first political party with a broad popular support, the *Sarekat Islam*, which stood in opposition against Dutch colonial rule.[12] These confrontations between the Muslims and Western powers in the region must have made the British aware of the potential force of the religion against colonial rule. It is not surprising, therefore, that the image of Islam and the extent of its influence on Malay laws were subject to ideological distortions. Instances of the writers' negative assessment of Islam that we have

[12] For an account of Dutch colonial policy on Islam, please refer to Harry J. Benda. 1958. *The Crescent and the Rising Sun*. Pt. 1. The Hague: W. Van Hoeve Ltd. See also the discussion by A. Naquib Suminto. 1985. *Islam di Indonesia: Politik Hindia Belanda*. Singapore: Pustaka Nasional.

shown earlier reveal their ideological bias. An even more glaring instance is Raffles' assertion (1835: 94) that Islam is a robber religion. Such a statement, made without considering the universal and humanitarian values of Islam, constitutes evidence of such bias. This negative image of Islam and problems arising from its impact on Malay laws were consistently reiterated in colonial scholarship.

Apart from this, the writers also sought to establish that Islamic influence on Malay laws generally, is superficial and nominal. Such an attempt at portraying the view that Islam's influence is not incisive but akin rather to a foreign element grafted upon Malay adat is evident in Wilkinson's study. Utilising the law of marriage as an illustration, Wilkinson notes,

> the average Malay looks upon marriage as true religious ceremony such as a French father looks upon the civil procedure which validated a marriage, it is sufficient for legality but for nothing more. The true Malay wedding ceremonies lie outside the Muslim law; the henna staining festivities, the bridegroom's procession, the mimic fights, the ceremonial ablution of newly married pair—all these prominent features of a Malay marriage belong to an older law than that of Shafie. A wedding before the religious authority is like a marriage before the Registrar; it is tolerated only. A Malay would consider that his daughter had disgraced herself if she was satisfied with a marriage before the local kadi (Wilkinson, 1908: 51–52).

Wilkinson fails to grasp that Islam itself accommodates these customs since they do not oppose its teachings. Though these originated in pre-Islamic times, Islam is neutral to these practices. It neither explicitly allows for nor prohibits their persistence. Furthermore, to imply that these customs represent the true living law of the Malays is misleading. Today, it is becoming common for Malays to forgo many of these marriage customs without any public outcry, though the same cannot be said with dispensing the religious aspect of marriage that determines its validity. Even if such a development may not have taken place during Wilkinson's time, nevertheless the illustration is relevant in revealing the aspect of the adat regarded by the Malays as eternal as opposed to the elements considered changeable.

More vigorous attempts at portraying the view that Islamic influence on Malay law is superficial are also manifested in the writings of Hooker. The basis for his judgment lies in the persistence of certain "pre-Islamic" features of the legal digests. According to Hooker, these reveal diverse cultural and religious sources of the law. Thus Hooker asserts, "It is notable that the Islamic ethic did not carry all before it. Our literature of the Islamic era retained very many features of the pre-Islamic period as indeed, Muslim belief in Southeast Asia still does today . . . The legal manifestations of Islam are thus highly culture specific as to time and place. One cannot suppose the triumph of *fiqh* either generally or in any particular area. Thus, for example, the (celebrated) Terengganu inscription, which is variously dated at sometime in the fourteenth century derives the authority of law from God but uses Malayo Javanese concepts to describe it. This multiplicity of source and variety of cultural and religious reference coexisting in the same document is typical of the digests as a whole" (Hooker, 1984: 9). Hooker's perception of the superficial influence of Islam on Malay laws is further conveyed as follows: "Histories are Islamic or not, mostly not, with Islamic colourings which are either historically improbable or ephemeral and the same is true of the Legal Digest" (page 4).

Hooker's evaluation is misleading. He concludes that Islam merely colours the legal digest, for instance, the Terengganu Inscription, on the basis of the incorporation of certain alleged pre-Islamic terms. Hooker fails to take into account the operation of fundamental sociological rules in the process of integration of new elements within an existing culture, which is relevant in understanding its manifestations in the realm of law. One scholar's opinion is instructive on this point:

> . . . any religion, philosophy, science, art or language when adopted by a people is always interwoven with their pre-existing cultural heredity. Bolshevism in Russia contains pre-Marxist Russian elements, Christianity in Europe is soaked with pre-Christian cultural traits, Islam in Malaysia, Arabia and other parts of the Muslim world is intermingled with the cultural legacy of the respective countries. During the initial period of conversion the influence of the pre-existing background is usually stronger than at the later phase. This is a general sociological law which should not thrill us as if it were an important discovery (Alatas, 1962: 242).

Applying this insight to the sphere of Malay laws, the fact that in the preamble of the Terengganu Inscription, the Supreme God which calls on the rulers to adhere to the rules inscribed is referred to as "Dewata Mulia Raya" in no way implies that the influence of Islam on the Inscription is but a superficial cloak on the largely Indian and indigenous beliefs, as Hooker strongly asserts. It is not inconsistent with Islam that God is referred to in these terms so long as the unique conception of the Unity and Oneness of God is understood and accepted. Even the term Allah was used to refer to a Supreme God in pre-Islamic Arabian society. After the coming of Islam, the term Allah persisted though the conception of Allah differed radically between the Muslims and the Arabs of pre-Islamic times (Gibb and Kramars, 1953: 33–41). A mere reference to a term which couches a conception of God without understanding the meaning of the conception cannot then be used to justify the belief that Islam did not deeply influence Malay laws.

An extension of such incorrect thinking is further evident in Hooker's appraisal of the significance of certain terminologies in the Inscription, such as "dharma". He perceives the persistence of such terms as revealing a number of "legal worlds". For Hooker, the term "legal worlds" differed from "legal ideas", which, according to him, does not adequately portray its meaning. Thus he comments, "the inscription, incomplete though it is, we find a number of legal ideas or, more accurately, a number of legal worlds" (Hooker, 1976: 129). Contextually, it suggests that terminologies in the digest reveal distinct and separate worldviews. Hooker lists these as Islamic, Indian and Southeast Asian. He further adduces that it is the last and not Islam or Indian influence which determines the substance of legal ideas. Thus he asserts that Islamic and Indian elements "while decisive for structure and form, must not be taken as determining the substance of Southeast Asian legal history. The genius of Malayan law lies in its ability to synthesize foreign elements and yet remain true to itself" (page 131).

Yet, mere terms found in the Inscription do not reflect "legal worlds" in the sense intended by Hooker without taking into consideration the context in which the terms were utilised. The term "dharma" used by Hooker to reflect the Indian legal world is one such instance. In Hindu usage, *dharma* refers specifically to the religious, moral, social and legal duties which pertain to the various castes and to all men (Kuppuswami, 1986: 6). Yet the intimate connection of *dharma* to the duties imposed on the castes finds no support in the Terengganu Inscription. Thus the term can only be sensibly understood if it is interpreted loosely to mean law. Contextually, the term dharma refers to Islamic law and the teachings of the Prophet Mohammad. In much the same way, the term '*hukm*' which referred to the laws of pre Islamic Arabic tribes and which continued in usage after the coming of Islam cannot be taken to imply a pre Islamic legal world (Schacht, 1964: 77).[13] This is because, '*hukm*' began to mean a particular set of rules and obligations based upon the teachings of Islam, many of which were contrary to pre Islamic hukm.

The "Southeast Asian legal world", Hooker denotes partly by the existence of rules in the Inscription which he believed parallel those found in later Malay law texts (Hooker, 1976: 130). Again this argument in explaining away the pervasive influence of Islam is flawed. It fails to acknowledge the fact that the later Malay law texts have been influenced by Islam. In fact, these were written only after the coming of Islam. To conclude that these rules are distinctly Southeast Asian is indeed fallacious. On the whole, there is stronger support for the view that the laws of the Terengganu Inscription are Islamic. To interpret otherwise is inconsistent with the content of the preamble of the Inscription which enjoins obedience to Islamic law and the teachings of the Prophet (page 128).

The writers' attempts at dismissing the profound influence of Islam on Malay laws reveal a more fundamental problem. Underlying this notion is the wider and deeply rooted opinion that Islam did not deeply influence Malay beliefs. This view cannot be dichotomized from the specific problem of perception of Islamic influence on the laws. Perhaps the most pronounced evidence of such thinking is found in Hooker's writings. In his article entitled a "*Note on the Malayan Legal Digests*", Hooker (1968: 160) explicitly postulates the superficial influence of Islam on Malay beliefs as follows:

> . . . In any religious contact situation, there is often an attempted syncretism between aboriginal religious beliefs and the doctrines and rituals of (in this case) Islam . . . In the study of the dynamics of religion one of the remaining problems is to discover more systematically the conditions under which a contact situation of this type may lead to a nativistic reaction of some kind or, at the other end of the scale, a response to syncretism. Even where a supposed conversion response to Islam has taken place, it may be nothing more than a syncretic reaction which takes over the outer forms of Islam but retains the inner and deeper meanings of native religious practices and value system.

[13] On the term *hukum*, please refer to Schacht, 1964: 77.

Hooker's conjecture that there may be no deep transformation in the belief system of the Malays with the coming of Islam is neither original nor is it isolated from the earlier general thinking of scholars on Islamisation in Malaysia. One scholar has pointed out that such views originated from Snouck Hurgronje and Van Leur, whose perceptions laid the foundation for the belief that Islam was merely a thin veneer on the massive body of indigenous civilization. This supposition has been dismissed as but vain conjecture (Alatas, 1962: 225–27).

Hooker himself did not explicitly base his view on these "authorities." Nevertheless, his assumptions reveal a perpetuation of such postulations. The spill over of this thinking into the realm of law is evident. Hooker's assertion of the multiplicity of "legal worlds" in dealing with the Terengganu Inscription is a manifestation of this notion. It is this assumption that Islam did not deeply influence Malay beliefs from which Hooker derives his judgment that the influence of Islam on Malay laws is a superficial one.

Hooker also believed that the legal influence of Islam on the Malays was superficial. This is conveyed in his argument on the causes of assimilation of Islamic elements in the legal digests. According to Hooker, it was the political factor which was the main reason. Islam was incorporated merely to serve the ideological interests of the ruling class. Thus he asserts: "The holders of power, the rulers were Muslims and to them the Legal Digests were both an affirmation of power and a definition of sovereignty. The result was an Islamised law text" (Hooker, 1984: 4). Hooker's emphasis on ideological motives is again evident in the following quote: "In many cases the aim of an obviously Islamic text in which fikh is prominent (e.g. the later Malacca recensions) was to legitimize the position of the text patron by reference to his prerogative as an Islamic sovereign" (page 34). Even in his earlier work on the Terengganu Inscription, Hooker had maintained this position. The Islamic elements in the Inscription were believed to have served only as a definition of sovereignty (1976: 130).

Hooker's account of the causes for the introduction of Islam into adat laws of the Malays reveals inconsistencies. He failed to take into consideration the reasons why the sovereign, in order to seek legitimacy, sought recourse to Islam. Unless there was already growing recognition for the introduction of Islamic law, there would not have been a necessity to legitimize their rule on the basis of Islam.

Only if such is the case can we perceive an advantage that can be gained by the rulers in introducing Islamic laws.

Furthermore, in attributing the reasons for legal change to a single cause, Hooker commits the mistake of over generalizing. He did not pay sufficient attention to the fact that aspects of Islamic law may have been adopted as an inevitable effect of genuine conversation involving both the people and the ruling class. As Gibb explains:

> every legal system presupposes that those persons to whom it applies are willing to recognise its authority and acknowledge it as binding upon them, even though they may, from time to time take the risk of contravening its specific injunctions. The acceptance of Islamic law then, was conditional upon the acceptance of the religion of Islam but it also followed inevitably from the fact of becoming Muslim. The religion of Islam was accepted by a large number of societies, each of which had a long social and legal tradition of its own. In adopting Islam as their religion, the members of those societies also accepted in principle the authority of Islamic law (Gibb, 1975: 88).

Similarly, another scholar explains:

> Submission to the law is at the same time a social duty and a precept of faith; whosoever violates it, not only infringes the legal order, but commits a sin, because there is no right in which God has not a share. Judicial order and religion, law and morals, are the two aspects of that same will, from which the Muslim community derives its existence and its direction; every legal question is in itself a case of conscience, and jurisprudence points to theology as its ultimate base (de Santillana, 1949: 288).

Hooker's argument that the persistence of "*non fikh*" and "*anti fikh*" elements in the laws of the Malays reveal their lack of conviction of the laws is misleading. That some such elements persisted after the coming of Islam is undeniable. This is because the old legal traditions inconsistent with Islam cannot simply be abolished at one stroke. Furthermore, the phenomenon cannot be effectively understood without taking into account the interests of significant social groups which hamper or obstruct the process of eradication of unIslamic features of the law. For instance, Hooker failed to consider the ideological interests of the ruling class in ensuring and justifying the perpetuation of specific laws which served to establish their power in the Malay feudal social structure. Some of these laws have already been mentioned earlier (pages 53–54).

His argument suggesting that the law was introduced as a definition of sovereignty and nothing more, raises yet another problem. It assumes that they were enacted by or originated from a monarch ideologically motivated to legitimize his authority through this means. Yet pertinent studies have thrown serious doubts on the generality of such assumptions. One scholar, for instance, has warned against the unfounded assumption by historians that the Terengganu Inscription originated from a monarch (whom the historians have not identified), on the ground that relevant knowledge of the social sciences has not been applied to the interpretation of this digest. Applying the findings of psychology of religion and sociology to the problem of sequence of religious conversion in Southeast Asia, the author maintained that the Inscription probably stemmed from the work of pious enthusiasts (and not the ruler), who exhorted the others to follow the path of Islam in the name of the ruler (Alatas, 1964: 2–4).

Yet another attempt at explaining away the significance of Islam on the laws of the Malays is manifested in Hooker's argument on the ways in which the digests acquired authority. He subscribed to the view that the authority of the digests rested upon two essential grounds, namely, their written form and their reference to an absolute source. Thus in discussing the "sovereignty" of these digests, Hooker asserts,

> I am not using the term in its modern sense of state sovereignty; . . . the reference is to the mechanism on which the generality of the Legal Digests founded their justification, starting with the mere fact of being reduced to writing. This effectively distinguished them from local and oral custom and it also made them largely unintelligible to the local population; a process of mystification, by means of writing in a special language had set in.

Hooker then adds,

> the reference to a foreign source, a source absolute in nature and powerful in political expression . . . tended to validate the contents of the Digests. This is a validation by association, a form of justification common in Southeast Asia where genealogy and descent have traditionally been used to legitimize rulers and kingdoms. In these cases, the fact of reference is of itself decisive; this was often misunderstood, especially by nineteenth century commentators, who sought an explanation in that which was referred to rather than in the act of reference itself (Hooker, 1984: 34).

Both these arguments are puzzling and absurd. Hooker assumes that because the laws are written, and therefore differ from oral tradition, they are unintelligible. What is worse is the implication that it is the very unintelligibility of the law that justifies its "sovereignty". Logically, the fact that laws are written does not imply that they cannot be comprehended. Many Muslims today cannot read the Quran but they nevertheless understand the laws embodied therein. Knowledge of the Quran can be and has been transmitted in numerous ways that facilitate understanding. Similarly, the laws embodied in the digests could have been comprehended despite the fact that many were unable to read them. Verbal expositions of the law by individuals and institutions such as the Sufi orders, is one of such means (Al-Attas, 1969: 26–27). There is nothing mystifying in all this. On the contrary, it is Hooker's reasoning that is mystifying. Furthermore, if it is the fact of reference that is decisive and not what was referred to, why is a particular conception of God, namely the Islamic one as opposed to others, invoked?

The perception that the influence of Islam on Malay laws is superficial could have stemmed from inadequate knowledge of Islam. This shortcoming is revealed in Hooker's attempts at delineating the Islamic content of the legal digests, namely the *Undang-Undang Melaka.* Due to Hooker's scant knowledge of Islam, innumerable provisions of the digest which bear the unmistakable influence of Islam were overlooked. Only those which make explicit reference to the words "Law of God" were pointed out as Islamic. Hooker is like one who sees only the dominant black spots on the vast expanse of material.

Take, for instance, Article 1.3 of the *Undang-Undang Melaka,* which according to Hooker, is amongst those provisions which do not distinctly reflect Islamic influence. This article stipulates the attributes of a ruler as follows: "The qualities required of a ruler are four in number. Firstly, (he is) merciful, secondly (he is) generous, thirdly (he is) courageous and fourthly (he is) able to give his verdict decisively. These are the qualities required of a ruler from time immemorial until the present day. This is what is understood by kanun law" (Liaw, 1976: 67).

Admittedly, the words "Law of God" do not figure in this provision. However, this does not mean that the provision is not Islamic. Even if the notion of the sound attributes of a ruler existed prior to Islam, they are consistent and in harmony with the spirit and content of Islamic conceptions of leadership. Islam enjoins that rulers be compassionate, merciful, generous, magnanimous, tolerant, courageous and just towards their subjects. Islam also emphasizes that rulers must inculcate a good sense of judgment. They are also warned against oppressive conduct which would incur the hatred of their subjects (Jafri, 1984: 625–47).[14]

Another clear instance of Hooker's failure to grasp the Islamic elements in the digest is manifested in his failure to perceive as Islamic, Article 23. This provision deals with the validity of agreements concluded under extreme circumstances:

> If a land is at war or a natural disaster has hit the land and its dignitaries and all the people . . . are suffering from hunger because of a shortage of provisions and all the people who are poor and destitute and people from the low classes and the religious mendicants are saying "Take us as your slave, give us food. If we were given food, you may later sell us." And they are given food by those who have food in reserve. After some time when the famine is over, the providers of food wish to sell all those to whom they have given food and the latter . . . make a complaint to the judge, the judge will not allow those people to be sold because when (they) agreed (to enslave themselves), . . . they were in an emergency (Liaw, 1976: 117).

Similarly Article 23.3, which invalidates agreements made between rescuers and people shipwrecked at sea, whereby the latter agrees to serve as slaves or even be sold to the former; this is not perceived by Hooker as Islamic, which in fact it is, being as they are consistent with the spirit of Islam (page 119).

Although, according to the Quran, a contract is a source of obligation and its faithful fulfillment a duty, yet these principles are subject to several qualifications. The Shariah does not recognize as valid agreements that violate the principle of reasonableness, even if the legal formalities of the contract are satisfied. Thus, both Shafie and Hanafi jurists dismiss as invalid agreements between consenting parties that result in excessive gain or undue advantage by one at the expense of the other, irrespective of any element of fraud (Kadduri, 1955: 193). By analogy, the provision of the Malacca Code falls within this exception. Furthermore, the provision is also in harmony with the teachings of Islam in the sense that Islam considers it a duty to assist those in distress. The Quran stipulates this clearly in

[14] For a discussion on the qualities of a ruler also see Al-Ghazali's *Counsel for Kings*. 1964. Translated by F.R.C. Bagley. London: Oxford University Press.

the following verse (S11 Verse 177): it is righteousness . . . to spend of your substance, out of love for Him, for your kin, for orphans, for the needy, for the wayfarer, for those who ask and for the ransom of slaves; to be steadfast in prayer, and practice regular charity . . .

Failure to determine the evident influence of Islam also occurs with respect to Article 34 on trusteeship (Liaw, 1976: 147). The ethical principles underlying this fiduciary relationship such as due care and probity revealed in the digest, are in consonance with the moral precepts enjoined by Islam of trustees in the management of trust property. The trustee's duty according to the Quran is to faithfully guard the contents of the trust and to render it back when required (S11, Verse 283). Trust property should not be usurped nor are trustees allowed to "misappropriate their trusts" (S1V, Verse 58). Hooker, however, fails to identify these provisions as embodying strong Islamic precepts.

In a recent journal on the theme of 'Islamic Law in South-East Asia', Hooker provides yet another revealing instance of the persistence of this perspective albeit with some modification. In the introduction, Hooker maintains that, to understand the influence of Islam on what he calls the "premodern Law texts", one needs to understand the idea of "purposeful selection which characterizes Southeast Asian law." Local recipients, he maintains, select the Islam that they find relevant to their local culture and contexts but not at the expense of their belief and identity as Muslims. It is the local and cultural forms that determine what Islam meant or how the faith is culturally defined. Thus one can speak of 'Islams' although there have been movements from within to minimize cultural variations which have existed for centuries. Examples he cited include the *Undang-Undang Melaka* which, according to him, reveal that only marriage and divorce are recognizably derived from Islamic sources while, those dealing with debts and property rights, for instance, are based on adat. Furthermore, the diversity of three sources of law stipulated in the text, namely, reason, Islam and customs of the country, justify his view that Islam was not the only source of law. Hooker even added, albeit without justification, that, "where there is conflict or inconsistency, (between these sources) then the Islamic element is ranked lower than the other two" (Hooker, 2003).

As we have earlier maintained, there is no doubt that with the spread of Islam into the Malay archipelago, Muslim legal traditions were inevitably assimilated and interwoven into pre-Islamic legal and cultural traditions of the receiving group. For instance, pre-existing feudal laws doubtless remained, due to the ideological interests of the ruling class and the protection of their power and authority. However, to assume that this process brought about a separation of legal realms which, in the case of conflict, would render Islam a subordinate position, reminds one of the presumptions of earlier scholars like Wilkinson. Hooker, however, clearly did not identify with the 19th century European scholars of that age of high imperialism for, according to him, they saw the texts as a corruption of a "pure" Islamic law given the indigenous rules contained in it (Hooker, 2003). Yet Hooker himself falls into the same conceptual pitfall, as he presupposes an Islamic law distinct from local, culturally specific laws. His presumption that substantive law covering broad areas of property and contractual agreements were adat simply because they do not expressly indicate an Islamic source attests to this fact. In this sense, like the colonial predecessors, he too assumes a "pure" Islamic law foreign to native law largely because he fails to see that the very indigenous law he highlighted had been influenced by Islamic principles or were not incompatible with them. Similarly his assumption that reason and custom mentioned in the legal texts as sources of law, are distinct from Islam, reveals yet another problem of perception. As far back as the beginning of Islam, reason and custom have been upheld and later developed by many prominent jurists as valid sources of law (cf. Masud, 2001).[15] Hooker misses the fact that Islamic law, like any other living law, is dynamic, and incorporates the customs and practices of a given culture in which it evolves. Consequently, he does not identify adat laws as bearing the influence of Islam unless they explicitly mention the word Islam or reveal a source he deems Islamic. This leads him to conclude misleadingly that the influence of Islam is confined only to selected aspects like marriage.

Gross inaccuracies on Islam and Islamic legal history also prevail extensively in some of these writings. Though they may not directly bear upon the issue of adat, they nevertheless reveal limitations in the writers' knowledge of Islam which inevitably affect the credibility of their studies. It is not the author's intention here to deal

[15] For a more current discussion of this issue refer to Muhammad Khalid Masud, *Muslim Jurists' Quest for the Normative Basis of Shariah: Inaugural lecture.* ISIM, Leiden, 2001.

exhaustively with such inadequacies for there are far too many. A few, however, need to be highlighted to substantiate our argument. The assertion by Wilkinson of the basis upon which the Quran and *hadith* are determined immediately comes to mind. According to the author,

> textual criticism was a very simple matter in those days. The present text of the Koran was arrived at by the prohibitive expedient of preserving only the manuscript and burning all the rest while the choices of these hadith or "tradition" came to be decided more by dream and prayers rather than by the weight of serious evidence (Wilkinson, 1908: 46)

These remarks imply that the contents of Islamic law were derived by irrational and arbitrary means. Such a baseless speculation reflects the author's lack of understanding of his subject matter. If Wilkinson had been a serious scholar, he would have been more cautious than to commit such blatant errors. Though unsubstantiated, Wilkinson's opinions nevertheless reveal a close resemblance to the views propounded by authors on Islam as far back as the twelfth century which have been severely criticised (Danial, 1960: Chap. 1).

Gross inaccuracies are also evident in Wilkinson's view on how the validity of the *hadith* was determined. Such views were made oblivious of the works of the prominent Muslim jurists including Hanbali, Hanafi, Shafie and Malik, who devoted their minds to the development of systematic, rigorous and precise methods of legal reasoning in determining the authenticity of *hadith* literature.[16]

Yet another manifest misconception about Islam is revealed in Wilkinson's remark that Islamic ideas of jurisprudence differed from those of the English in that the former, unlike the latter, does not separate the executive from judicial power (Wilkinson, 1908: 65–66). This perception again reveals a lack of knowledge of the legal history of Islam. Although at the beginning, there was no clear distinction in the functions of government, yet subsequently, under the reign of the Caliph Umar, this distinction was institutionalized. Justice was administered by judges who were independent of the Governor. Umar was the first ruler to fix salaries for judges and to make their

[16] An account of the growth and development of the science of *hadith* literature is substantially discussed by Joseph Schacht in his book *The Origins of Muhammadan Jurisprudence* (1975).

officers distinct from those of the executive (Ameer Ali, 1899: 62).

Even more glaring is Wilkinson's erroneous understanding of the nature of Islamic law, though the remark may have been intended as a credit to the law. The following assertion illustrates this point: "Mohammadan law . . . is theoretically unchangeable. A ruler may supplement but he cannot alter the law of the Prophet, however, unjust the law may seem. It is a great tribute to the virtues of Muslim jurisprudence that ten centuries have not made it out of date" (Wilkinson, 1908: 67).

Wilkinson is perhaps unaware of the fact that Muhammad himself had, from the very inception of Islam, made a distinction between what he believed as revelation, coming from a supernatural source, and ideas which were the products of his own mind (Watt, 1953: 52–58). This therefore means that not everything the Prophet ruled should be taken as immutable. Furthermore, prominent Muslim jurists concur that Islamic law is capable of change and modification to suit different social conditions. As one scholar succinctly states:

> It is not unchangeable and depending on mere tradition. The great schools of law agree on this point. "The legal rule" say the Hanafites "is not unchangeable; it is not the same as the rules of grammar and logic. It expresses what generally happens and changes with the circumstances which have produced it". "Law is also liable to change with regard to its application. Malikites and Hanafites agree on this point . . . The Arabs have perceived very clearly the reason for this flexibility. It is again usage. Societies are living organisms and undergo ceaseless change during their life . . . when society becomes wealthier more numerous precepts were multiplied. This continuity of life may be seen in the course of Islamic history." (De Santillana, 1949: 305).

At times, scant knowledge of Islamic history leads to absurd conjectures. For instance, Wilkinson believed it a striking feature of Islamic jurisprudence that a man learned in the law is forbidden to seek office as a judge and is even directed to refuse should the post be offered to him. Thus, according to Wilkinson, "It is not for a mere whim that the great Arab jurist Abu Hanifa, suffered scourging and imprisonment rather than become a kadi. The Muslim ideal was that the study of divine law should be absolutely free from the taint of self-seeking" (Wilkinson, 1908: 67).

These utterances reveal not only a complete ignorance of Islamic history but also the precepts of Islam. Islam does not enjoin asceticism. Historically, prominent jurists refused judgeship because they revolted against the immorality and injustices of the ruling class. The latter's excesses drove away scholars from serving in the rulers' entourage. In view of the abuses in the exercise of authority by the ruling class, suspect from the religious point of view, many religious scholars preferred exile, imprisonment and public whipping to government service (Goitein, 1966: 205).

Conclusion

This chapter has presented the thought and opinions of adat law writers on the theme of Islam and its relationship with Malay adat laws. Some of their misconceptions have been pointed out, as well as their fallacies in judgment and inadequacies in evaluation. These stem essentially from an insufficient knowledge of both Islam as well as adat laws and a strong bias against the former. Such overgeneralizations, faulty perceptions and unsubstantiated presumptions that permeate colonial scholarship on Islam bypass the norms and standards of intellectual discourse thereby seriously impairing a more objective understanding of the influence of Islam on Malay laws.

CHAPTER FOUR

ADAT LAND AND INHERITANCE LAWS

Studies on Malay adat laws were not only confined to questions on the nature and sources of the law, as portrayed earlier in the preceding chapters. Given that the writers were essentially colonial administrators, an equally if not more important aspect of their writings concerned their attempts to conceive specific rules of adat, particularly those which facilitated colonial administrative functions and which directly coincided with the interest of colonial capitalism. Of these, perhaps none has been more amply discussed than the question of land tenure and inheritance.

Two of the foremost British colonial administrators whose perceptions of and opinions on Malay land tenure were of major significance in determining land legislation in the Malay states were W.E. Maxwell and F.A. Swettenham. Their elaborate studies are generally considered as authoritative by subsequent writers on adat land laws.

Attempts at conceptualizing Malay land tenure were consciously determined by two factors. One was the practical concern of colonial rulers with the need to raise revenue from land to maintain the colonial machinery. Another conditioning factor was the interest of colonial capitalists for whom such studies were relevant particularly with respect to the powers of Malay proprietors to alienate land (Maxwell, 1884: 77). The collusion of interests between these two significant groups in Malay colonial history conditioned the writers' understanding of Malay land tenure.

What then was the writers' conception of Malay land tenure? Generally, both Maxwell and Swettenham believed that, in a Malay state, land belongs to the ruler (Maxwell, 1894: xiv). Maxwell, for instance, reveals his opinion as follows:

> It is not difficult to see how the rights of the Raja to demand a proportion of the produce, on pain of forfeiture of the holding, and to dispose of waste land, tended by degrees to create the doctrine that the right to the soil was in the Raja. Such a doctrine did in fact grow up and being to all appearance, consistent with the rights exercised

> by the Raja and not incompatible with the proprietary right claimed by the Malay landholder, it has received complete acceptance in the Malay States . . . That the soil of a Malay State is vested in the Raja is a doctrine not now to be questioned . . . (1884: 90–91).

Serious implications arise from the perception that ownership of land is vested in the ruler. They pertain to the nature of the Malay subjects' proprietary interest in land. Swettenham, for instance, maintained (Maxwell, 1894: xiv) that land in the Malay states did not belong to subjects, who only had a usufruct of the land: "the Malay cultivator was not the owner of the land he occupied, that he was a tenant at will and that whether he remains in occupation or not depended purely on the caprice of the Malay ruler." This position is further reinforced by Swettenham's assertion, in the case of Perak, that:

> Before 1874, there was no such thing as 'national tenure' in Perak, the Malays possessed no proprietary rights over the land, that no land can be said to have descended to them from their forefathers and that while the Rulers never admitted any claim to the land on the part of the people, these last never advanced any such claim but frankly stated as they do now that land belonged to the Kerajaan, that occupants were tenants at will and that all the claim they had was to the 'usaha', the usufruct of the ground. I have taken a great deal of trouble to make certain that what I say is right. I have questioned the Sultan, the Dato' Temenggong and other chiefs, the better classes and orang rakyat . . . They never fail to say that the land belonged to the State and never to the occupant, that the cultivator could claim and sell his crop or his house but had no title to the land and that in as much as the land did not belong to them they never paid anything for it nor could they dispose of it. They all equally agree that everyone sat down where he pleased so long as the local penghulu allowed him and that as a rule they continued in undisturbed possession of whatever they chose to cultivate, the land being abundant (Maxwell, 1894: xiv).

While Swettenham denied that the Malay cultivators possessed proprietary rights to the land, Maxwell proclaimed otherwise. Essentially, Maxwell perceived that the Malay proprietary rights to land were created by the clearing of land followed by continuous occupation. Once this was satisfied, the cultivators' right was absolute, subject to two conditions. These were the payment of a tax constituting one-tenth of the produce from the soil, and the performance of compulsory service to the sovereign (Maxwell, 1884: 77–90). Like Swettenham, however, Maxwell defined the Malay cultivators' proprietary interest in land as no more than a "usufruct" (Maxwell, 1884: 91).

Furthermore, he also perceived the legal position of the Malay peasant as a tenant, as is revealed in his following assertion: "Tenant right is the cardinal doctrine of the Malay cultivator and as long as that is fully recognized, it does not matter to him who or what functionary or power may, in theory, be clothed with the original and supreme right to the soil" (Maxwell, 1884: 92).

The notion that absolute ownership in land is vested with the Malay ruler thereby qualifying the Malay subjects' rights as merely the usufructary rights of a tenant, may have been conditioned by certain events in history affecting British claim to land and hence revenue derived from it. In fact, contextually, Maxwell's theory of Malay land tenure was expounded partly in response to the problem of determining the interests of Dutch grantees in Malacca, though Maxwell himself intended his theory to be of general application to the Malay states (Maxwell, 1884: 92–97).

When the British took over Malacca from the Dutch in 1825, it was found that scarcely a foot of the land, with the exception of a few spots, belonged to the government. The Dutch had granted proprietary right to the soil of the whole territory of Malacca to various individuals. These concessions had been passed by descent or transfer into the hands of persons who now claimed against the British administration full title to the lands (Newbold, 1839: vol. 1, 162). Though there were many technical grounds upon which the British attempted to nullify the Dutch grantees' claims, none perhaps provided more effective a solution than the justification on the basis of supposed Malay land tenure. In effect, therefore, the theory that all land belonged to the sovereign legitimized the denial to Dutch grantees of any proprietary claims to land. The argument essentially was that because all land belonged absolutely to the ruler, the grantees possessed merely the rights and privileges to collect the tithe and ensure the performance of services to the raja. They could not claim ownership of the land.

Apart from this particular concern, the conception that Malay land tenure gave the sovereign absolute ownership of the soil may have also been conditioned by the ideological interest to promote colonial capitalism. It is evident that land was the most valuable asset in the Malay states. The most convenient way by which land could be opened and utilized for purposes of mining and agriculture was by propagating the theoretical justification that all land belonged to the king.

The supposition in effect meant that the British, through the institution of the residential system, could determine the disposal of land as they deemed fit. As one author succinctly states:

> Land, then the only asset of the country, was really what the colonial government was after. The potentialities of its use and development for mining and agricultural exploitation could see no limits but the boundaries of the State. That the new government should have full ownership in and power of disposal over the vast no man's land could not therefore have been subject to any question. Whether it was the exact position under the indigenous system of land tenure, it was simply taken for granted by the colonial government that all lands in the State must belong to the Sultan. Maxwell's theory about the indigenous land tenure, though advanced about a decade after Perak and Selangor had succumbed to British protection, actually represented an attempt at a theoretical (and purportedly) sociological account in confirmation of the presumption as to the Sultan's absolute ownership of all lands which had in fact been acted upon by the colonial officers. It may be added that as the Sultan was regarded as the absolute owner of all lands in his State, it followed that he had power to grant or otherwise deal with his land and to make new laws relating to land matters. And what the Sultan had power to do, the British Resident could do in his name. Therefore as a political fact and also in theory as it was accepted, the colonial government in the protected Malay States had a free hand to offer their lands to the world of private ownership in any form that would suit capitalist enterprises (Wong, 1975: 23–24).

That the assumption served as an important ideological tool to the colonial power is further reinforced by the fact that Malay rulers did not actively participate in making laws relating to land use. They did not initiate land legislation. Though enactments relating to land were issued in their name, control over land matters remained effectively with the colonial power (Lim, 1976: 147–148).

In its historical manifestations, the theory legitimized grants in the Federated Malay States (FMS) to British capitalists for mining and agricultural plantation. Some of these included long term leases accorded on the most liberal terms and cheaply apportioned.[1] In Perak, when efforts to attract investments from these capitalists proved

---

[1] For a detailed classification of the types of land, terms and conditions of leases and their rents, please refer to The Land Laws and Land Administration in the FMS, pp. 1–2.

disappointing, the government generously allowed thousands of acres of virgin land for plantation agriculture to be leased to British capitalists in perpetuity. Land that had been granted to these capitalists before indirect rule was established, such as in the case of Pahang, the colonial government confirmed these grants so long as capitalists could show that they had reasonable prospects of working effectively or cultivating continuously within the time for which the concession had been granted. Thus the theory that land belonged to the ruler served the ideological interests of colonial administrators like Swettenham who favoured a free hand system guided by the philosophy that the government should deal liberally with men who were ready to invest their money (Lim, 1976: 90–94).

The theory also benefitted the British in yet another way. It meant that territories could be alienated by the simple and convenient devise of treaties between the Malay ruler on the one hand and the British on the other without the fetters of individual claims to the soil. Historically, such an assumption has ensured the transfer of entire territories to the British without much inconvenience, as witnessed in the case of Singapore.

The colonial capitalistic ideology that justified British monopoly over land matters also ensured the provision of substantial benefits for the Malay ruling class. In this way they generally succeeded in curbing their dissatisfaction or antagonism resulting from the loss of effective political power. Malay elites were offered large areas of land at nominal costs and through a variety of other devices. In Perak, for instance, the sultan was granted 1000 acres of land while in Larut the chieftains were allowed to collect a tax of 10 per cent on all produce exported on irrigation canals between Sungei Nibong and Sungei Buaia in Lower Perak for twenty years. Substantial incentives were also accorded to them in administering land matters. For example, they were entitled to collect a percentage on the value of certain produce of the district (*mukim*) in addition to being granted land free of assessment and quit rent during their term of office (Lim, 1976: 147–151). In Negri Sembilan, when land registration was introduced, chiefs agreed to accept allowances either a fixed amount or percentage of revenues in commutation of their share of the proceeds of alienating vacant land. The most enduring of these arrangements was that which gave the chiefs of Rembau the right to one third of all land revenues. Thereafter, vacant land became state land (Gullick, 1951: 44).

It is pertinent to note that neither Maxwell nor Swettenham relied upon relevant aspects of Malay adat laws in their attempts to portray Malay land tenure. This may have stemmed from the fact that none of the provisions in the Malay digests that discuss the question of land clearly conveys that absolute ownership is vested in the sovereign. The following provision of the *Minangkabau Code of Perak* is a case in point. It expresses the view that abandoned land belongs to no one and can be appropriated by any person, for it has "gone back to God":

> In the case of a farm which has been abandoned, that is to say, where a man has felled and cleared forest land and then has allowed his property to go back to the jungle, ye must by no means permit any opposition on the part of the former cultivator to its appropriation by another for it is land which has reverted to the jungle. Ye must not suffer the former owners to dispute possession, for the field has gone back to God, and custom declares that there shall be no such dispute.

Support for this argument is also found in the *Perak Code*. The article which explains the right of a person to clear forest land reveals the assumption that the forest belonged to no man: "The law regarding the clearing of forest land . . . Such land becomes the property of the person who clears it, subject to two conditions, first he must be a Muhammadan; secondly, the land must not be already in the possession of another person" (Maxwell, 1884: 171, 173).

A similar conception of ownership in land is also found in Article 16 of the *Laws of Kedah*, which states the following: "In the case of dead land, which is land which bears no signs of appropriation, such land belongs to God. As such, the ruler has possession of the land. If there are signs of appropriation, the land belongs to the owner . . ." (Winstedt, 1928: 31).

This article clearly expresses the principle that unappropriated land belongs to God. It also implies that anyone who so wishes to clear and cultivate it can do so, whereupon the land then belongs to him. Therefore the phrase pertaining to the ruler's possession of the land can only be taken to imply that the ruler has only a custodian role in relation to land.[2] To construe it to mean that the ruler owns the

---

[2] The conception that land does not belong to the ruler who has only a supervisory and custodian role in relation to it also exists in other colonized societies. For examples, please refer to Elias, 1956, 164–165. See also the discussion highlighted by M. Gluckman, "Property Rights and Status in African Traditional Law"

land is clearly inconsistent with the clear wording of the article that secures ownership to anyone who appropriates it. The meaning of this article can perhaps be more clearly understood in the light of traditional Malay society in which the ruler was regarded as God's representative on earth.[3] Theoretically, this conception of kingship implied that the ruler is delegated and entrusted with the administration of the kingdom and all that is found in it. In view of this, it is not unreasonable to maintain that the ruler is merely a trustee and custodian of the land.

The above evidence also reveals that Swettenham fails to understand the perception and sentiments of the Malays when they assert that land belongs to the king. Such an assertion interpreted contextually must be taken to mean that it is by the bounty of the king as custodian of land that the subjects are allowed productive use of it. It is his good grace that ensures Malay peasants their right to land by clearing and cultivating it.

In fact, it may even be argued that the very notion of absolute ownership of land that Maxwell and Swettenham ascribe to the Malay ruler is misleading. This is because, whenever the issue of ownership is treated in the Malay legal digests, it consistently reveals a close connection with the effort at appropriating the land. The conception of ownership portrayed in the digests is one indivisibly tied to a function performed on the land. Ownership ceases once the land no longer shows evidence of clearing and cultivation. Apart from the above provisions, support for this view can also be found in the *Undang-Undang Melaka*. The following article, which discusses the law relating to "dead land" and "living land", provides a good illustration of this point. It states that:

> With regard to dead land, nobody has property rights to it, (when) there is no sign of its being under cultivation by someone, . . . If someone cultivates it . . . no one can proceed against him . . . Concerning "living land", here there are signs of ownership be it a well or trees

in *Ideas and Procedures in African Customary Law*, ed. by M. Gluckman, Oxford University Press, London, 1969, pp. 256–257.

[3] See, for example, the *Sejarah Melayu*, W.G. Shellabear (ed.), Penerbit Fajar Bakti, K.L., 1979, p. 141. The argument that a ruler has only a custodian role in relation to land based upon Islam finds support in the discussion highlighted by Ahmad Nazri Abdullah in his book *Melayu dan Tanah*, Media Intelek, K.L., 1985, pp. 8–13. On the Islamic conception of the ruler as vicegerent of God on earth, please refer to Al-Ghazali's *Counsel for Kings*, trans. by F.R.C. Bagley, Oxford University Press, London, 1964, Pt. 11, Chapter 1.

> whose fruits are for consumption or other signs of its being under cultivation. If a man makes a compound or builds a house . . . or cultivates it . . . he is open to public criticism and may even be sued for the land (in question) is known as "living land". If he trespass upon (such land), he shall be fined . . . (Liaw, 1976: 111).

Such rules of adat are instructive. They clearly show that the idea of absolute ownership of land, devoid of any evidence of its productive use or occupation does not feature in the land laws of the Malays. As such, the authors' attempts to ascribe to the ruler ownership of land irrespective of these elements are unconvincing.

The notion of absolute ownership of property irrespective of the function element was prevalent in England in the era when the modern industrial system took shape. The view meant that an object that became a proprietary right is absolute. The institution of property invokes the right of the owner to use it or refrain from using it as he pleases and its principal significance was to supply him an income irrespective of any duties or social functions which he may discharge (Tawney, 1920: Chapter 4).[4] Maxwell's perception of the absolute ownership of land of the Malay ruler discloses these traits.

It is also reasonable to suspect that Maxwell's and Swettenham's characterization of Malay peasant's proprietary interest in land as a mere usufruct, may also have been influenced by this dominant perception of property. Accustomed as they may have been to the idea that rights over property once established are inviolable, the authors were unable to define accurately the interest of the Malay peasants. They did not conceive that rights over land could belong absolutely to the cultivator and yet may lapse to another who appropriates it, once it no longer bears signs of use.

The term 'usufruct' utilized to describe the proprietary interest of the Malay peasants is inappropriate and misleading. It does not convey the strength of their interests in land. Meek, in his book *Land Law and Customs in the Colonies*, has drawn attention to the dangers of the indiscriminate use of Western concepts to define ownership in the colonised societies (Meek, 1946: 11). Though Maxwell himself cautioned against the uncritical utilization of Western concepts

[4] For some insights into the historical variations in the conception of property in the West, see the discussion highlighted by K. Mannheim, *Essays on Sociology and Social Psychology*, Routledge and Kegan Paul, London, 1953, pp. 104–105.

in describing Malay tenure, nevertheless, he suffers from this shortcoming. Technically, a usufruct is defined as the right of using and enjoying property belonging to another provided the substance of the property remains unimpaired. One who enjoys the usufruct must refrain from using the property for a purpose other than that agreed upon, nor alter its character, and is bound to restore it when impaired. Furthermore, he who has the usufruct cannot legally transfer it to another and though he may let or sell the use of it, he continues to remain responsible to the owner. When the usufruct ends, the property reverts to the owner (Pritchard, 1964: 213–214). None of these elements which characterize a usufruct apply to Malay rights in land as evident in the digests. Land in the Malay states was not another's property and as such, was not inevitably bound to revert to the owner. Furthermore, land could be transferred and may also devolve upon one's descendants.

This implies that the Malays have a proprietary interest in the soil that was permanent and transmissible, unlike that of a usufruct. Adat inheritance laws such as those found in Article 33 of the *Ninety-Nine Laws of Perak* render support for this view since only a more permanent proprietary interest in land necessitates a systematic law of succession (Hooker, 1970: 66). The existence of laws of inheritance also proves wrong Swettenham's assertion that Malay subjects having only a usufruct to the land cannot claim to have land "descended to them from their forefathers."

Maxwell also attempted to base his thesis that ownership was vested in the ruler upon certain incidents of tenure that he alleged were enforced upon Malay subjects. These were the mandatory payment of a tithe and the performance of forced services for the ruler (Maxwell, 1884: 90, 110). His argument is, however, marred by the absence of adequate and reliable evidence that the compulsory payment of a tithe was actualized in the Malay states. In fact, this practice was emphatically denied by Swettenham whose disagreement with Maxwell is summarised as follows (Maxwell, 1894: xiv):

> . . . that in Perak, (and also in other Malay States) it never was the practice for cultivators to make any payment for the use of land and that to speak of the payment of tithes as an immemorial Malay custom was simply to make a mistake.

Such a position is further strengthened by the fact that Maxwell himself relies on but vague and speculative arguments in support of his claim. He maintained without ample evidence that the right of the sovereign to demand a tithe, the failure to pay which would result in the seizure of land, was introduced into the Malay states by Hindu rulers (Maxwell, 1884: 89). Furthermore, Maxwell himself admitted that the only area in which he witnessed the tithe imposed was in Krian, a district that however belonged to the personal estate of the sultan (Maxwell, 1884: 97–98). As a result of the limitations and inadequacies of his argument, Maxwell's attempts at establishing the general thesis that the sovereign has a superior proprietary right to the soil, that he in fact owns the land, is unconvincing.

The argument that Malay peasants' proprietary rights are subject to compulsory incidents of tenure is not only utilized by Maxwell to support the view that the ruler owns the land. Such allegations of the limitations of the rights of the subjects in relation to land are equally significant to the interests of the colonial power in yet another way. It attempts to ensure that a land revenue system is justified based on the traditional laws of the Malays themselves. In this way, not only would such a conception produce the necessary resources to maintain the colonial machinery, it would do so in ways that would minimize criticisms against colonial economic policies.

Inconsistency in arguments also arises with respect to the issue of the tithe. While arguing that this practice was introduced by Hindu rulers from India, Maxwell simultaneously attempts to justify this rule on the grounds of Islamic law. The following assertion in his *Memorandum* (Maxwell, 1894: x–xi) illustrates this point:

> The Malays are Mohammedans and with their faith have acquired the principles of Mohammadan law . . . that the tithe is a Malay, in the sense of being a Mohammadan institution . . . is perfectly well-known to the Malays of the Peninsula and treated of in their books and that Malay land tenure is generally founded upon Mohammadan law.

Maxwell's attempts at invoking the supposed rule of the Shariah is also a consciously selective one, utilized only when it suits the interests of the colonial power and can be used as a justification for its policies. For instance, he did not take into effective consideration the provision in the *Perak Digest* which stipulates that one of the conditions which must be satisfied in order to acquire a proprietary interest in land is that the individual must be a Muslim.[5] This principle

[5] *The Perak Code*, in Maxwell (1884: 171).

finds its source in the Shafie school of law as seen in the legal opinion of al-Nawawi.[6] Yet it is evident that Maxwell ignores this condition. He was not opposed to the introduction of European systems of tenure that allowed for European capitalists to acquire interests in land.

The argument expounded by Maxwell that the Malay cultivator is subject to a mandatory payment of a tithe failing which he would be dispossessed of his land, a doctrine Maxwell asserts is based upon Islam, is erroneous. In fact, this view is a gross misrepresentation of Islamic law and reveals a failure to grasp the spirit of welfare that underlies it. Although Islamic law imposes a payment of a tithe constituting one-tenth of the actual produce of the soil on Muslim cultivators, there is no evidence to indicate that non-payment would result in the owner being dispossessed of his land. After all, the objective of the tithe is to aid the needy (Hamilton and Bensley, 1985: vol. 2, 210). As such, Islamic law takes into consideration reasons for failure to comply with the tithe. It provides exceptions to the general rule in cases that justify its alleviation. For instance, if the tax cannot be met because the crops are destroyed due to a bad harvest or for reasons other than the fault of the owner, the law exempts him from payment. Furthermore, the needy are exempt from the tithe. More importantly, there is no evidence whatsoever to suggest that if the holder fails to comply with the rule even if it was due to his own fault, such non-compliance entitles the ruler to forfeit the land. At most, evidence indicates that the landholder continues to be responsible for the tithe which becomes a debt for which he is responsible and must be paid out of the general assets of his estate (Baillie, 1953: 12–13, 27).

Maxwell's understanding of the condition for continued proprietary rights in land with respect to the tithe is unfounded for yet another reason. It brings to question his conception of customary land tenure in relation to the Malay social structure. In feudal Malay society, the political power and prestige of the ruling class was dependant upon the progress and prosperity of the villages. Revenue from the villages was used to support the ruling elite and their following.

[6] Nawawi, *Minhaj et Talibin: A Manual of Mahammadan Law according to the School of Shafie*, W. Thacker, London, 1914, p. 226, "Every believer may by clearing it, appropriate any piece of land situated in a Moslem country that has never been cultivated or built upon. Infidel subjects of our sovereign do not enjoy this right".

Failure to ensure that the territory within their control was sufficiently prosperous would result in the possibility of being ousted by a rival since this would mean that the ruler lacked the means to support an adequate force to maintain his position. As such, even if the ruler were a despot, he would not have allowed his subjects to be deprived of land out of a failure to pay the tax, since the maintenance of his very power and prestige depended upon their well being (Gullick, 1958: Chapter 7).

A comparable reciprocal relationship existed in English feudal society between the lord and his tenants who occupied land for generations and whose eviction or forfeiture of land for failure to pay rents was never generally practiced. The prominent historian Tawney, explained this lucidly:

> The feudal seigneur had at his worst been a lawless tyrant, and at his best a despotic parent. But he had governed his estate as the sovereign, often the resident sovereign of a petty kingdom, whose interests were roughly identical with his own, and though his depredations were a terror to his neighbours, his own tenants had little to fear from them, for his tenants were the force on which his existence depended (Tawney, 1912: 191–92).

Tawney's analysis of the changes to the social significance of land that had hitherto characterized feudal agrarian relations is also instructive. The causes he ascribed to these changes were never witnessed in traditional Malay society. Essentially, the scholar attributed these changes to the imposition of the system of enclosures on land in the sixteenth century by a new class of businessmen who, having made their wealth in trade, began investing in landed estates. With the "instincts of a shopkeeper", they removed peasants from land which conflicted with their interests when they, the peasants, could not meet their dues or when their tenancy expired. As Tawney submits (1912: 192–93),

> . . . But the men of business, and the men of fashion and the patrons of literature, are alike in being the symptoms of a new economic and political system, a system which has shorn landownership of the territorial sovereignty which had gone with it, broken down the personal relations of landlord and tenant, and by turning agriculture into a business, has made it at once more profitable and less strenuous for the former, more exacting and less stable for the latter, than it had been when a landlord was not only a drawer of rents but a local sovereign, a tenant not only a source of income but a dependant who was bound by a tie which was almost sacramental.

The significance of land in relation to Malay social structure perhaps explains why Malay customary laws do not provide evidence that sanctions such a practice. It is pertinent to note, according to the Malay legal digests, that one is still entitled to ownership of one's land even if one flees from the village because one had incurred the wrath of the sultan. In Malay feudal society, this was indeed a very serious offence. *The Undang-Undang Melaka*, for instance, is instructive on this point:

> With regard to rules relating to a village which has been deserted: If someone settles in it, eats the fruits thereof and sells them he can be sued by the owner . . . The same ruling applies to all who have come under royal wrath and have fled the country for fear, leaving their villages and compounds deserted; they as owners can sue the occupant because it is their property by right . . . if someone informs the judge . . . the judge shall order that it (the property) be returned to the owner. Such is the law (Liaw, 1976: 109).

This article is significant in so far as it reveals that even in the event of what is regarded as a grievous offence in Malay feudal society, one is still allowed the proprietary right to one's land. In the light of such evidence, Maxwell's arguments pertaining to forfeiture of land due to non-payment of the tithe are unconvincing.

Furthermore, where Malay adat laws sanction expulsion from the village (which implies that one loses the right to one's land), this occurs only with respect to social rather than economic misdemeanors. For instance, the *Ninety-Nine Laws of Perak* prescribe expulsion from the country as one of the modes of punishment imposed on those who commit adultery and/or improper sexual conduct (Hooker, 1970: 75).

Yet another manifestation of the failure to grasp the social significance of land is evidenced by the fact that both Maxwell and Swettenham failed to take into adequate consideration the communal aspects of land ownership. The omission, consciously or otherwise, mars a comprehensive and accurate understanding of the nature of Malay proprietary rights to land. This dimension of ownership is of such immense significance that it has never escaped the attention of scholars in their studies on the land tenure of diverse native societies.[7] The phrase "communal aspects of ownership" does not

[7] For some examples, please refer to M. Gluckmann (1969: 252–63); Meek (1946: 16–27); Ter Haar (1948: chapters 2–4).

mean that the community shares proprietary rights of the individual in land. On the contrary, evidence thus far reveals that what is acquired by the individual's active participation in land through clearing and cultivation belongs to him. Nevertheless, it is only by the affirmation and consent of the community that the individual is entitled to establish legal relations with the land. The community also regulates the rights and obligations of individuals within it as well as against outsiders. Furthermore, it is the community that determines and imposes limitations on land use and regulates the powers of disposal of land (Ter Haar, 1948: 81–94).

One of the significant consequences of avoiding this aspect of Malay land tenure, is the failure to take into account its effect on the power of the individual to alienate land or to engage in land transactions with outsiders. For instance, in many Malay states, members of a different cultural group were not always welcomed into a village to which they did not belong (Gullick, 1958: 26). This strongly implied a limitation on the power of disposal of land. An individual would not be encouraged to sell or pledge his land to a stranger or an outsider without the prior agreement of the villagers and chiefs. Furthermore, the right of pre-emption to members of one's kin who usually resided in the same village would generally be upheld as against strangers and outsiders (Gullick, 1958: 32–34).

Neither Maxwell nor Swettenham took into effective consideration this pertinent aspect of ownership. Although Swettenham mentioned the fact that the Malay in order to occupy land required the permission of the village chief, he failed to pursue the significance of this prerequisite. Maxwell was no more enlightening. In his discussion on alienation and other transactions involving land, this salient feature of Malay land ownership is simply absent. Maxwell was preoccupied only with establishing that the Malay cultivator could transfer his land. His concern then lay in determining the value of land upon alienation. In a way, the lack of consideration for this aspect of land tenure may have been conditioned by attempts to reduce fetters on land transactions and the power of the colonial authorities to deal freely with land. As Mannheim (1976: 246) aptly explains,

> even in the formulation of concepts, the angle of vision is guided by the observer's interests. Thought, namely is directed in accordance with what a particular social group expects. Thus, out of the possible data of experience, every concept combines within itself only that which,

> in the light of the investigator's interests, it is essential to grasp and to incorporate . . . the absence of certain concepts indicates very often not only the absence of certain points of view but also the absence of a definite drive to come to grips with certain life problems.

Swettenham's proposals to introduce a system of ownership rights in land based on the instrument of title in return for an annual ground rent involves a complete eradication of Malay land tenure (Maxwell, 1894: xiv). The substitute was a modern land tenure system foreign to the Malays where ownership was based on a system of registration of title. Swettenham may have been perceptive to grasp that the adoption of the Malay conception of tenure would provide obstacles to colonial capitalism since it offered various problems. For instance, Malay land laws are embedded with fetters on alienability and there is no secure title. Furthermore, since rights depended on actual cultivation, boundaries of land and one's proprietary rights could fluctuate. The absence of clear boundaries, written records and the flexibility of the system were incompatible with the demands of the colonial government to ensure a consistent and well defined land revenue system. Furthermore, these characteristics of native land tenure obstructed the easc with which land could be disposed of for purposes of plantation agriculture and mining—the cornerstone of British economic policy.

Empirically, the introduction of modern land tenure such as that expounded by Swettenham in the Malay states did not benefit the interests of the Malay subjects nor enhanced their welfare. The overall result caused by the direct impact of the introduction of alien concepts of land as well as the discriminating attitude of British officials in the implementation of the law led to dire consequences such as indebtedness and the gradual loss of land belonging to the Malays. This system made it possible to own land as absentee landlords. Such an arrangement favoured those with capital especially the European capitalist community, which had the backing of capital and some local entrepreneurs with capital in mining and commerce. As for those Malay subjects without capital, any further acquisition of land was almost impossible. In fact they became victims of large-scale absorption of land by planters and planting companies leading to loss of ownership of land. Lim Teck Ghee's pertinent observation on the effects of the introduction of modern land laws in Perak is instructive:

> In practice however, the introduction of the modern tenure in Perak and in other Malay States, worked to the detriment of the Malay. As early as 1879, there was an indication of the manner in which the Malay was deprived of a meaningful participation in the development of the country in which he, more than any other community or group except perhaps for the aborigine, had an interest and stake. Ironically it was Swettenham, the main architect and principal proponent of the alien tenure in Perak who noticed that Kho Bu Ann, a Chinese sugar planter in Krian "by the right of might and money, had absorbed into his sugar estate a number of properties to which Malays of his district had a prescriptive claim." The loss of Malay land rights was hastened by the discreet discrimination practiced in some official circles against the Malay peasant cultivator. This was done by allotting the more valuable tracts of land to Europeans or other planters and by pushing the Malay peasant to land which was less valuable . . . While such policies hurt Malay land interests badly, the colonial government's failure to ensure that the peasant community comprehended the modern concepts of land tenure it was introducing in the Malay States was damaging to the Malay agriculturalist. As a result, a situation rapidly arose whereby Malay landholders who possessed neither the will nor the means to resist unscrupulous lawyers and money lenders were exploited (Lim, 1976: 157).

Inheritance

Yet another aspect of property that has received considerable attention from colonial writers is the law governing its distribution. With the institutionalization of an English judicial system, questions of inheritance hitherto arbitrated by traditional village chiefs came to be determined by British judges and officers. The essential problems faced by the latter were in deciding what the law of succession practiced by the Malays was, and giving effect to that law. The problem, however, was not simply a legal one for in so determining the law, their conceptions were conditioned by their preferences, bias and understanding of adat law.

It is in this light that we attempt to appraise the perceptions of E.N. Taylor, a prominent member of the colonial service who showed some concern in portraying and evaluating adat inheritance laws. Taylor's studies suffer several essential drawbacks. Taylor reveals misguided perceptions of the relationship between adat and Islam which has implications on his understanding of both adat and Muslim inheritance laws. Misconceptions of the *faraid* also abound in his writings.[8]

Taylor's approach to the study of Malay inheritance law is misleading and reveals salient traits of Orientalism. Of relevance here is the tendency to resort to reductionist arguments in discussing the impact of Islam on the changing adat law of inheritance. For instance, he fails to take into consideration the effects of significant social and economic developments, which have conditioned and influenced the gradual evolution of adat, apart from Islam. In his writings, Taylor shows a preoccupation with Islam as though Islam were the only significant force of change affecting adat inheritance laws, in particular that of the adat Perpateh. Yet this was certainly not the case. Several studies have shown that the adat Perpateh law on inheritance has been gradually transformed as a result of more incisive forces apart from Islam including Schrieke's in his *Indonesian Sociological Studies*. Though Schrieke's study is concerned with the more general changes of the adat in Minangkabau society in response to changing economic and social conditions, his study is instructive in so far as it deals with the effects of those forces of change on the gradual transformation of adat inheritance laws. In this respect, one of the major economic factors noted by Schrieke was the penetration of the money economy into what was hitherto a self-sufficient society. This in turn brought about individualizing effects upon the society, one of which was the strengthening of the bond between a man and his children at the cost of his relations. As a result, the adat laws of inheritance were slowly modified to suit these changing circumstances. Hence, whereas previously even the few goods a man acquired by his own efforts during his lifetime were surrendered to his family on his death, it was now possible for children to inherit their father's self-earned property by means of a gift or will (Schrieke, 1966: 95–143).

The Malay states were similarly exposed to some of these forces of change with a consequent impact upon customary distribution of ancestral property (De Jong, 1960: 165–166). Since the second half of the 19th century, increasing monetization of the economy saw a

[8] For a good account of Islamic inheritance laws, please refer to Syed Ameer Ali, *Mohammedan Law*, Vol. 11, Thacker, Spink & Co., Calcutta, 1917, Pt. 1.

shift from subsistence farming to cash crop production, particularly rubber. Market demands for these products led to commercialization of land. In Negri Sembilan these developments corresponded to a rise of disputed claims amongst kinsmen over the devolution of property such that by the 1920s there were already growing signs that villagers were reluctant to be subject to clan imposed restrictions on land use and transfer. The practice whereby acreage acquired by the joint efforts of spouses during the course of their marriage which hitherto, would have been deemed tanah pusaka (ancestral property) upon the transmission to their children, gradually declined. The situation contrasted with the traditional adat whereby a married couple's acquired property (*charian laki bini*) automatically became clan controlled ancestral property (*tanah pusaka*) as soon as their grandchildren if not their offspring inherited it. Moreover, it also departed from the past practice when land, not even deemed *tanah pusaka* was inevitably awarded to the female issue. These departures from traditional customs influenced by economic changes modified the traditional adat law on inheritance (Peletz, 1981: 32–37).

The change was reinforced by laws enacted by the colonial government. Beginning from 1888, laws were enacted permitting titles to be issued to individual villagers with the related aim of accumulating annual revenue. These laws radically transformed the traditional adat practice by enabling male villages to obtain legal title to cultivable plots of land independently of wives and related female kinsmen. Under the traditional adat law in Rembau, for instance, males were prohibited from inheriting property in the form of land although they could inherit moveable property such as cattle, weapons, and ornaments. It was also the British who institutionalized legal changes in 1893 to the effect that property of deceased persons in Sungei Ujong should no longer remain with or pass to relations on the female side, thereby tampering with traditional adat laws. These were introduced in spite of the policy arising from indirect rule that advocated non interference in matters of custom and religion. Arguably such policies served to ease land alienation and weaken clan ownership in the interests of colonial capitalism.

It is possible that given this context of socio-economic changes, the Islamic law of succession or *faraid* and other modes of property devolution recognized by Islamic law such as gifts or will which allowed property to devolve on one's offspring, spouse and others may have been viewed as a more meaningful or relevant alternative. Taylor, however, failed to grasp that the influence of the *faraid* cannot be understood in isolation from the impact of social forces that continuously modify and change the traditional adat societies. Lev provides an instance of this when he supports the view that when patterns of family organization have begun to change in response to changing economic conditions, Islamic inheritance rules may serve the function of supporting the new pattern. This is because with the rise of nuclear families instead of the traditional adat house, parents are more inclined to devolve property directly to their children who would have to make it on their own rather than to the family guardians (Lev, 1972: 193). It is, however, pertinent to point out that by accepting this argument, we do not rule out the fact that many Malays, being Muslims, accept the *faraid* as a part of their belief. We only seek to show by recourse to this argument that Taylor's failure to analyze forces of change on the adat, apart from Islam, limits his perspective of the problem.

Taylor personally favours the adat as opposed to Islamic inheritance laws. This is manifested in his attempts at preserving the adat, even at the expense of the demands by adat authorities that acquired property (*harta pencarian*) devolve according to the principles of the Shariah. None of the arguments he expounded to forestall the resolution of the *lembaga* is convincing and objective, as the following reveals: "I knew . . . that the Dato' had some such idea in his mind . . . the then Dato' Rembau was receiving . . . the stupendous income of about £3000 per annum and he had acquired considerable interests in new rubber land. In the event of divorcing his wife he would, if the ordinary rule of adat, *chari bahagi* applies to a ruling chief, have been compelled to give up half of this property to a woman with whom he had quarrelled. He had therefore a strong personal motive for trying to bring about a change of adat on this particular point" (Hooker, 1970: 190). Apart from the Dato' Rembau, Taylor also believed that the *lembaga* were generally motivated by personal interests; that they were, according to him, "speaking for themselves—not for their tribes" (Hooker, 1970: 191). Taylor was also of the opinion that, by their very authority, the *lembaga* could not decide anything outside of the adat (Hooker, 1970: 191). He therefore implied that changing the inheritance laws was a usurpation of the *lembaga's* authority.

Taylor's reasoning is marred by wild speculations and unfounded claims. This is especially the case with his first argument. The second ground which imposes a limitation on the powers of the *lembaga* to amend inheritance laws is baseless. Such a constraint is alien to the adat laws of Negri Sembilan. Although there are certain elements of the adat which are regarded as eternal because of their continued relevance to society, yet there is no evidence to support the view that this particular law of inheritance falls within the ambit of the exception. On the contrary, the inevitable fact of legal change in response to changes in social life is explicitly acknowledged in the sophisticated laws of Negri Sembilan (Winstedt and De Jong, 1954: 42).

Taylor also argues for the retention of the adat based on assumptions of the lawmakers' ignorance of the consequences of their resolutions on the application of the Islamic law of inheritance:

> There is a further and very important point which is not apparent from the face of this resolution. These lembagas are not educated men and what they say can only be rightly understood with reference to their own knowledge and background. They are the chiefs of exogamous tribes, steeped in those traditional sayings in which custom and religion are often confused. When they said they wanted acquired property to devolve according to religious law, although they still wanted ancestral property to devolve according to the adat Perpateh . . . it is clear that their dominant idea was this: 'We do not want Charian to be subject to restrictions on transfer, though we do want to maintain those restrictions on ancestral property.' Further, I have little doubt that they also meant 'we want charian to devolve on the sons and daughters of the marriage.' I am however quite sure that they did not mean that they wanted the charian of a man who had been married twice to devolve on all his children of both marriages because that would mean that a given piece of land would descend into two different tribes. The Mohammadan law is founded on patriarchy. The adat Perpateh is the purest matriarchy extant. The whole existence of the lembagas as chiefs depends on maintaining the integrity of the matriarchal tribe. It is utterly unreasonable to suppose that the lembagas meant to initiate a policy leading to their own abolition. Yet if the first part of the resolution be divorced from its context and followed literally, it would eventually bring about that result (Hooker, 1970: 191).

In effect, Taylor's reasoning reveals an attempt at establishing a superior knowledge of laws which were the creation of the Malays themselves and which they had protected, consciously developed and modified over centuries. Furthermore, it is the *lembaga* who are the guardians of the law. They are the legitimately constituted authority of the people to assume the role of ensuring the viability of the law. For Taylor, to assume that he knows better the laws and its implications than the guardians of the law themselves reveals his superiority complex. Like other colonial rulers of his time, Taylor assumes that his level of understanding and knowledge of Malay culture, religion and laws are superior to the Malays who practiced them. In a way, his assertions are part of the wider ideological attempts by the colonial power to denigrate the image of the native rulers and hence justify and legitimise the perpetuation of British rule. This is done even at the expense of portraying the Malays as too stupid, self-centered and ignorant of their own affairs to formulate an acceptable opinion. Taylor implies that his opinion constitutes a more valid and objective representation of what the people want and what they ought to have in their own interests (Hooker, 1970: 229).

Moreover, his argument reveals a static understanding of the adat. It is clear that with the introduction of Islam, the Malays in Negri Sembilan had come to accept as valid the marriage of a man to more than one wife even if they belonged to different clans. Since adat inheritance rules did not provide any solution to the distribution of property amongst children from wives belonging to different clans, it was only inevitable that adat be modified and adjusted to solve such problems brought about by changes in the beliefs of the society. Only when the adat fulfils this role can it be considered as a living law, one that is constantly relevant to the requirements of the society. On the other hand, to prevent the adat from undergoing the inevitable process of change is merely to strangle its evolution and retard its growth. Hitherto, the adat had remained relevant precisely because it had succeeded in modifying its rules to serve changes in the social conditions of the community.

The rule which allows for acquired property to devolve upon one's children is by itself an instance of the dynamism of the adat. Unless Taylor is unaware that the very rule of adat of which he speaks has evolved, he ought not to have perceived the adat as unchangeable. His attempts to protect the adat in effect merely preserves it by forcing it back into its groove without taking into consideration its capacity to resolve problems that have arisen within the society. As such, his conception, consciously or otherwise, serves only to divorce the adat from the society it regulated and to undermine its relevance.[9]

Taylor's static conception of the adat inheritance law may have stemmed from his uncritical reliance on Wilkinson's general perception of the relationship between adat law and Islam. His following assertion serves as evidence:

> . . . it is . . . absolutely necessary to acquire a clear idea of the different elements of the law which come into real or supposed conflict. Fortunately, we have at hand a monograph which is at once clear, concise and authoritative. I therefore invite every reader of this opinion to pause here and to read, or re-read the late Mr Wilkinson's Law—Introductory Sketch . . . It occupies only some sixty pages . . . but it provides the indispensable foundation of comparative law without which any intensive study would be built upon sand (Hooker, 1970: 162).
>
> Given this framework, Taylor submits that Islam and the adat "are really irreconcilable" (Taylor, 1937: 4).

This unquestioning reliance on Wilkinson as the legitimate expert on Malay jurisprudence regardless of what the Malays themselves think, manifests the mode in which Orientalism as a style of thought operates. Consistent with how Orientalist literature establishes its peculiar authority as depicted by Said, Wilkinson is established as the eminent authority, a source of knowledge on scholarship on the laws of the oriental Malay whose work is not only particularly effective but effects to dispose of pre-existing knowledge on the subject. Invoking him serves as part of the process of the creation of a lineage or a family of ideas that gains prestige by continued reliance. But as Said argues, "yet if this gain coincided with a loss in originality, we should not be entirely surprised, since this mode, from the beginning, was reconstruction and repetition" (Said, 1978: 122).

Conditioned by such a perspective, Taylor's perception of Islamic law like that of the adat is static. Preconceiving it as a distinct and radically different system of law from the adat he cannot recognize its dynamism in accommodating and absorbing adat law consistent with its values and spirit. Thus Taylor does not grasp the mutual influence of Islam and adat law in the matter of inheritance even in the face of clear evidence to the contrary. Instead, he weaves these into his preconceived notions. A clear instance arises with

[9] M. Natsir provides an interesting argument to this effect in his book *Capita Selecta*, Bulan Bintang, Jakarta, 1973, pp. 170–171.

respect to distribution of property with the consent of heirs practiced in the Malay states. This arrangement is allowed in Islam (Ameer Ali, 1917: 53).[10] Yet Taylor chooses to perceive otherwise. He asserts:

> The fact that the Muhammedan law allows distribution of the estate of deceased persons to be settled by consent of the heirs has enabled many arrangements which were in reality applications of kampong custom to pass as distributions according to Muhammadan law and has therefore been beneficial in individual cases but it obviously tends to confusion of thought and has in fact led to much misunderstanding and the use of misleading terms (Taylor, 1937: 10).

In effect however, it is Taylor himself who misunderstands the issue.

Yet another instance which reveals the mutuality of Islam and adat inheritance laws but which Taylor explicitly denies given his conflict perspective occurs in the case of *harta sepencharian*. This is a rule of adat which allows a woman upon divorce, a share of property acquired during marriage out of the joint efforts or joint resources of both herself and her husband. The share varies in the different Malay states between one third and half. The Malays themselves generally do not perceive this rule as conflicting or departing from Islamic principles in violation of their faith. In fact they view it as part of the Islamic law. The principle by which the Quran allows a widow the right to property belonging to her either before her marriage or which she acquires during the marriage irrespective of her legal entitlement to a fraction of the deceased's estate, provides basis for recognition of *harta sepencarian* as compatible with Islamic law (Qur'an, IV, 32). Muslim jurists as expert witnesses in cases of dispute before the Shariah court also perceive this concept of adat law as analogous to *harta sharikat* or partnership property which is subjected to division upon divorce; in recent times this concept has been articulated as synonymous with the concept of *musha* which refers to the properties of husband and wife that have been mixed up.[11] Taylor however, consciously or otherwise misrepresents the problem. Dichotomizing Islam and the adat, he maintains: "They are unable to distinguish in principle between Malay custom and Muhammedan law and they will confidently propound as a provision

[10] Refer also to Ahmad Ibrahim. Islamic Law in Malaya. Malaysian Sociological Research Institute, Singapore, 1965, p. 246.

[11] Mansjur bin Abdul Rahman v Kamariah bte Noordin [1988] 3 MLJ xlviii.

of Muhammedan law a rule which is really a rule of adat" (Taylor, 1937: 9).

Taylor's static conception of adat law is further revealed in his failure to perceive the significance of pertinent instances revealing the gradual acceptance of the *faraid.* He fails to grasp the fact that these pieces of evidence, though few and isolated, are immensely significant in indicating that the adat is in a process of gradual transformation in response to the changing requirement and consciousness of the people. One cannot expect complete changes in the law over a short span of time as with the case of amending statutes. Nevertheless, these changes, though not pervasive, nor recognizable at first, reveal a process of evolution not effectively perceived by Taylor. As such, though Taylor himself is aware of such instances, he merely attempts to interpret them as minimal in influence. For instance, with respect to Rembau and Tampin, Taylor himself admits that in these areas "it may be doubted whether the tribal restriction would have been so well observed if they had not been reinforced by statutory procedure." Furthermore he also notes that from 1930 isolated cases of acquired land had devolved according to Islamic fractions (Hooker, 1970: 234). Yet Taylor misses the relevance of this data in throwing light on the dynamism of the adat in assimilating the influence of Islamic law.

The static perception of adat and Islamic law is also manifested in his discussion on *tanah pusaka* or ancestral property. This property is vested in the female members of the tribe, who hold it as trustees for their tribes. Contextually, his statements pertaining to tanah pusaka, strongly imply that they are irreconciliable with Islam. For instance, he submits that there is "no difference of opinion" that ancestral property devolves according to the Adat Perpateh, which as he had already determined at the outset, is wholly different from Islamic law (Hooker, 1970: 163, 191). His arguments reveal the notion that adat law and Islamic law are immutable, rigid and radically opposite categories which are irreconcilable. In this sense, Taylor fails to understand the dynamism and flexibility of the Islamic law governing devolution of property which has been developed by Muslim jurists and evolved over centuries in response to diverse social conditions and problems. For instance, the institution of *wakaf* recognized as valid amongst Muslim jurists reveals that Islamic law recognizes a category of property that is non-inheritable and non-alienable whereby beneficiaries may be allowed only a usufruct out of it. In this way the law has accommodated personal and community endowments as one of many modes of distribution of property (Powers, 1993: 379–406).

Without ample and prior studies on the varying rules of distribution in Islamic law, assertions made as a matter of course and unquestioned assumptions like those found in Taylor's writings, cannot be easily accepted. Such inferences imply that the Malays choose to uphold and cherish an institution which undoubtedly contradicts their religious teachings. They inevitably flow from the perspective as demonstrated in Chapter Three above that the influence of Islam on the lives of the Malays is superficial. However, such allegations fail to capture diverse interpretations pertaining to the validity of ancestral property from the point of view of Islamic law. Indeed, in Malay history, some scholars have long held the view that ancestral property is not unIslamic but analogous to wakaf which was justified on the following bases: that it served significant social and economic functions including that of conserving property for the collective use of the existing and future members of the clan or tribe; that it prevented unwarranted alienation of land; it allowed members of the tribe the benefit of earnings or proceeds arising from its use; was not unjust to males since the matrilocal marriage arrangement meant that they moved over to live and work on land belonging to the family of the wives without bringing in land to the marriage. The very persistence of *harta pusaka* in the generally religious-conscious Minangkabau community exposed to the influence of Islam at least since the 13th century if not earlier, was a further argument upon which rests the claim that the Malays do not perceive the institution as conflicting with their religious ethos. Moreover, though many local institutions and customs have been subjected to criticisms and eradication as inconsistent with Islam as seen during the Paderi war, its ethical basis has not been questioned until relatively recently.

Scholars who hold the above views do not deny the existence of differences of opinions on the issue. However they maintain that within the context of profound economic and social transformations of the late nineteeth and twentieth centuries and the increasing popularity of the Islamic law of succession and distribution, articulation for the Islamic law may take on the rhetoric of a supposed polarity between the adat and Islam, a tendency believed to have been reinforced by collective opinions of groups predisposed to certain religious orientations or ideologies.[12] In a way, Gullick (1949: 41–42) also made a similar observation on the Malay state of Negeri Sembilan. Referring to disputes amongst kinsmen over devolution of property acquired by married men independently of wives or sisters, he maintained that although these came about due to economic forces that disrupted the traditional adat tenure rather than divided loyalties over adat and Islamic inheritance provisions per se, the dispute was couched in terms of adat and Islam and their mutual incompatibility with respect to certain dimensions of inheritance.

Taylor's view on the conflict between the adat law governing ancestral property and Islam is one sided and misleading in so far as he fails to take into consideration other legal opinions that do not subscribe to this view. This one sided portrayal is then over generalized as depicting the position of Islamic law on the issue. In this sense, Taylor neglects the varied juristic interpretations of Islamic inheritance law that had developed in response to varieties of social structures and condition. In this way he reinforces the discourse on adat and Islam conflict.

It is perhaps pertinent to point out that *harta pusaka* itself is not rigidly fossilized. In fact adat law contemplates situations whereby ancestral property may even be forgone due to extenuating circumstances that have a direct consequence on the collective interests of the tribe. Under situations whereby utilization of earnings alone from *harta pusaka* does not suffice for the survival of the tribe, adat law uplifts well-defined constraints imposed against alienation of the property. Instances of these situations include the fundamental need to provide shelter for the extended family of the clan, the need to marry off womenfolk who have exceeded marriageable age, provision for funeral expenses of members of the tribe and the appointment of leaders. Other extenuating circumstances include the need to settle collective debts, maintain property in disrepair and restore the honour of the members of the tribe. When these basic needs are wanting, ancestral property can be sacrificed to fulfill them.[13] In other

---

[12] See, for instance, the reasoning of Professor Hamka in Mochtar Naim (1968), Chapter 1. See also the view of Hazairin, Pergolakan Pejesuaian Hukum Islam dengan Adat, Djakarta, 1956.

[13] For a thorough discussion of these issues, please refer to Amir Syarifuddin

words, *harta pusaka* may cease to exist when circumstances warrant it. Thus, adat law regulating *harta pusaka*, as with the case of *harta charian*, are not insulated from, and must inevitably respond to, changing circumstances.

Taylor's static image of the adat is reminiscent of the views and ideas of colonial administrators of his time. Such ideas may have had the effect of preventing the gradual evolution of the law. For instance, legislation was passed in 1909 with the object of preventing dealings in tribal land with those outside the tribes. The Enactment empowered the collector to inscribe the words "Customary Land" on titles held subject to custom. The endorsement on the title is conclusive evidence that the land is held subject to custom and all dealings and transmissions connected with the land are dealt under the customary tenure enactment.[14] While this law effected to preserve ancestral property from alienation it also shielded it from accommodating and adjusting to forces of change.

Yet another problem pertains to Taylor's evaluation of the relative merits of adat and Islamic laws of inheritance. In many respects his assessment is flawed due to his failure to provide an accurate representation of the latter. He subscribes to the view that Islamic law does not accord with the Malay spirit and sense of justice particularly with respect to the determined share accorded to women. Thus he asserts:

> It is a well known and most significant fact that where the family are able to agree on a division, the widow always receives more than the very small share of the estate which Muhammedan law allows her. This is due to practical wisdom prevailing over prejudice or legal theory. In the vast majority of Malay families, one-eighth would not provide the widow with subsistence. Clearly therefore the matter is one which is in actual practice regulated by Malay custom rather than by Muhammedan laws (Taylor, 1937: 10).

Taylor's representation of the Islamic law on inheritance with respect to women's entitled share is misleading. In fact, Islamic law by virtue of the fact that it allows a dying person to will away one-third of

(1984); Mochtar Naim (1968: 30–32). On the issue of sale of ancestral property in the Malay Peninsula, please refer to GA De C. De Moubray. Matriarchy in the Malay Peninsula and Neighbouring Countries. Routledge, London, 1931, p. 133.

[14] On the problems of the implementation of the law and its interpretation in courts, see the discussion of Ahmad Ibrahim (1965: 270–76).

his estate and dispose of it in a manner he deems fit, provides flexibility to the system. It makes it possible for a man to bequeath one-third of his estate to a wife or even a daughter in addition to her prescribed share. The only limitation of this right occurs when the bequest is made for purposes which are unjust or unlawful or when it robs the legal right of others to a share of the estate.[15]

Furthermore, Taylor also fails to take into consideration that in Islam, a widow is never cut off from the responsibility of her guardian, who continues to maintain and provide for her if she is unable to do so herself. Even if she fails to receive his assistance, the needy widow is entitled to seek financial assistance from the *Bait-ul-mal* or the property of the Muslim community and public treasury. Part of the contribution of Muslims towards this fund is specifically reserved for those who are in need of financial assistance and widows (Ameer Ali, 1917: 177–79).

Apart from the issue of fair distribution, Taylor's portrayal of the Islamic law of inheritance in relation to Muslim societies is clearly misleading. These societies are portrayed as nomadic communities in which land is not a popular form of property. This being the case the law is deemed to be unsuited to the agriculturally based Malay society. The fact that Islam spread over vast geographical regions encompassing diverse economies and cultural conditions is simply ignored. Thus he asserts:

> Law is not an abstract science. It has no real existence except in so far as it operates on the facts of everyday life. The law as laid down by Mohammed and his immediate successors had regard to the sociological conditions of the Arabs in their day and therefore important parts of it are concerned with marriage and divorce among tribes and families practicing patriarchy, polygamy and slavery. The most important kinds of property were camels and other flocks and herds, jewellery and money, land in Arabia being of relatively little value. The Muhammedan rules of distribution are therefore suited to the division of moveable property and are not apt for partition of land. The sociological condition of the Malays was and is entirely different. Agricultural peasants have few domestic animals and little money. The only important kind of property is land which is indeed essential to their very existence (Taylor, 1937: 5).

[15] For instances of the implementation of this law, please see N. Anderson, *Law Reform in the Muslim World*, Athlone Press, University of London, pp. 151–152.

Taylor further maintains that the rule of Islamic law, which he alleges requires division of property according to ascertained shares, though relevant to communities in which moveable property was most important, could not be made to apply to the Malay states without inviting harmful consequences. He cites fragmentation and subdivision of holdings, leading to impoverishment of land as a consequence of the adoption of the *faraid* (Hooker, 1970: 238).

The reasoning expounded by Taylor abounds with inaccuracies that reveal the level of his understanding of Islamic inheritance laws. His conception erroneously suggests that the laws were inapplicable to settled societies. Yet Madinah itself, the birthplace of Islam, was a prominent agricultural region. Furthermore, the existence of laws regulating the imposition of *zakat* (tax) on produce from land even during the time of the Prophet Muhammad is pertinent in revealing the fact that land constituted an important source of property upon which the livelihood of the people depended.[16]

Equally pertinent in illustrating Taylor's scant knowledge of Islam is his generalization that Islamic inheritance law leads to fragmentation and subdivision of land. He denies the reality that Muslim law has also developed other modes of transmission of property in response to different social conditions and needs. Taylor's assumption indicates a simplistic attempt to equate the Quranic stipulations of inheritance with actual practice without considering how laws have been developed by Muslim jurists over centuries to deal with a range of conditions without circumventing religious injunctions. Thus, from the very beginning neither the Prophet Muhammad nor his Companions allowed fragmentation and subdivision of land. As safeguards against this eventuality lands of the Medinites were protected from subdivision and alienation by entailment (*wakaf*) (Ameer Ali, 1899: 59). Furthermore, apart from endowments mentioned, bequests, personal arrangements based on unanimous consent and the like have long been practiced.

Although there have been more recent writings since Taylor's that have attempted to account for the forces that condition the increasing significance of the *faraid*, the conflict perspective between adat and Islam has not waned in influence. They attest to the authoritative paradigms of colonial scholars. Like the colonial writers, their

[16] For an account of some of these laws, please refer to Sharif (1963: 185).

works are based upon the presumption of a conflict between adat and Islam in the matter of inheritance laws. From this unquestioned presumption flow their arguments, and their conclusions endorse their premise. This approach is brought to bear in the work of de Josselin de Jong entitled *Islam verses Adat in Negri Sembilan* (Malaya) published in 1960. The work examined the debate that occurred in 1951 over the issue of distribution of *harta pusaka* involving the Religious Affairs Section (*Barisan Agama*) of the Rembau Branch of UMNO that had announced its plan of altering the customary law on the distribution of *harta pusaka* as codified in the Customary Tenure Enactment (Chapter 215) and bringing it into conformity with Islamic law. At the outset de Jong (1960: 159) reveals his conflict perspective asserting that:

> [from] birth members of Negri Sembilan's matrilineal clans are incorporated in an adat system which affects their persons and their property. At the same time, as Muslims, in a country which explicitly acknowledges itself to be an Islamic state, they must adhere to Islamic law, which in principle also claims an almost total authority over their lives, but which is *radically different* from the adat. Here lie the roots of the conflict that had its focus . . . in the differences between the two laws of inheritance.

The difference between the two systems, he maintains, "is great" and applies both to acquired and ancestral property. According to him, Islamic law, unlike adat, only recognizes individual ownership and not ownership of any kin group. It also goes against the adat's designation of individual heirs. Furthermore, it does not recognize the concept of joint property thereby having no rules for its division once property owning partnership is dissolved, unlike adat which regulates this upon divorce or death (de Jong, 1960: 161–62). In this sense, he reveals the continuity of thought of his predecessors, like Taylor, whom he explicitly quotes and relies upon in his essay.

Conditioned by this perspective, de Jong fails to consider the significance of the arguments he had collated as propounded by the adat representatives (whom he refers to as the traditionalists), to the effect that *harta pusaka* is not contrary to Islamic law. Essentially they justified its permissibility on the grounds that female heirs receive the land expressly as a gift (*hibah*) from those entitled to inherit it according to Muslim law such as her brother during her wedding ceremony. Furthermore, they also pointed out that all this while, religious officials have readily accepted *zakat* and *fitrah* (alms) from revenue derived from the land and have not questioned the practice of utilizing earnings from the land for religious rites including the performance of pilgrimage (*haj*). In addition, foundations or *wakaf* for the community's use have been created out of plots of *harta pusaka* without doubting its religious sanctity (de Jong, 1960: 172–73).

It is perhaps pertinent to point out that in summarising the arguments of the Islamic law advocates or "reformers" as he calls them, de Jong himself noted that "no specific reply ever seems to have been issued by the press by those who opposed this stance" whose weightiest argument, according to him, were that adat rules are *haram* or forbidden and therefore conflict with a Muslim's prime duty which is to avoid what is *haram* and practice what is *wajib* (compulsory). Even de Jong's categorization of the arguments of these opposing views by way of the "religious", "ethical" and "practical" considerations is misleading as it implies that the latter two aspects are independent of Islamic influence or content. Yet there is no basis to assume that issues discussed within these categories relating to questions of justice to male and female members of the clan or tribe or the social and economic significance of preserving ancestral land for the community's welfare is not devoid of religious consideration although Islam was not specifically mentioned in relation to these issues.

The debate showed clearly that not once did the "traditionalists" maintain that adat opposes Islam. On the contrary, they consistently expressed the sanctity of the Islamic law of inheritance while asserting that the distribution of ancestral property was not unislamic. This they argued by recourse to other legal devices and concepts recognized in Islamic law. Even their insistence that changes to the distribution laws of the community's property must be based on consensus, is not alien to the teachings of Islam. de Jong however missed the crux of the matter. Thus he characterised the debate as a conflict "between two systems of ideals and practices, both of which were considered by the society as integral to its culture, both applicable to the entire society and both perceived as a system by the inhabitants of that society" (de Jong, 1960: 199). On the contrary, the arguments, if followed objectively, reveal without doubt that both groups upheld only one ideal from which flowed different interpretations and practices. The conflict thus is not between ideals but how a single ideal based on Islam is understood differently by different groups of Malay Muslims. The factors conditioning these differences in standpoint may be due to adherence to different theological interpretations or ideological interests of groups within the social structure. de Jong did attempt to analyze some possible motivations and socio-economic factors for the articulation and demands for the imposition of Islamic law and adat by respective interests groups; however, we will not attempt to examine these here. Our aim is merely to reveal the fact that whatever may be these motivating factors they do not convincingly depict a polarity between adat and Islam. More importantly, both groups justified their stand by recourse to Islamic precepts whatever their ideological motives may be. de Jong's perspective of the 1951 controversy as one of conflict and tension between adat and Islam can be said to reveal the persistence of the conceptual framework of colonial scholarship on this aspect of adat laws.

Yet another manifestation of such a continuing perspective is evident in the work of Michael G. Peletz, an anthropologist well known for his works on the Negri Sembilan Malays. Our selective interest in his writings focuses essentially on the theme of adat and Islam specifically in relation to the question of inheritance. In his paper on *Social History and Evolution in the Interrelationship of Adat and Islam in Rembau, Negeri Sembilan*, Peletz started off by asserting that he intended his study to address what he sees as oversights and discrepancies in works on the Minangkabau society of Rembau including the domain of Islam which he maintains has "frequently been relegated to relative insignificance or discussed only in so far as necessary to substantiate one or another perspective on its articulation and status with respect to adat" (Peletz, 1981: 2). The author's perspective of the conflict between adat and Islam on this issue is revealed in his following assertion:

> Islamic texts . . . do not differentiate, as does adat, between harta pesaka and harta sepencarian (that is, between clan controlled "ancestral" property, on the one hand, and that which is "acquired" either jointly by spouses during the course of their marriage or by unmarried persons, on the other). Consequently, Islam permits inheritance practices and other aspects of property transfer forbidden by adat. In addition, Islamic sources do not recognize the concept of corporate land ownership, a concept of crucial importance in the agriculturally based adat system. As a result Islamic law not only disavows claims to property if they are based solely on membership in corporate kin groups but

> also regards certain adat traditions associated with property transfer as contrary to and forbidden by the Koran. Furthermore the legal conventions of Islam specify that a male child is entitled to receive inheritance shares in the proportion of two to every one share allotted to his sister. Adat, in contradistinction, while suggesting that all children regardless of sex deserve roughly equal portions of their parent's wealth, contains numerous provisions having the effect of prohibiting males from inheriting any property in the form of land (Peletz, 1981: 19–20).

Peletz's view in fact reveals the perpetuation of an unquestioned presumption of a static and rigid understanding of the two systems which he perceives as incompatible, distinct and contrasting, characteristic of colonial perspective. However, his arguments, unlike the views of some colonial scholars, reveal more sophistry than the simplistic, absolutely irreconcilable dichotomies like those found in the writings of Wilkinson. Peletz acknowledges that adat and Islam are compatible in several aspects overlooked by previous scholars. Utilizing adat sayings, he maintains that adat and Islamic teachings harmonize in advocating good values although he merely takes as a given without disclosing or demonstrating that the adat sources he utilized for comparison were indeed pre-Islamic.

It is apparent that Peletz's view stems from his perception of the nature of the influence of Islam on the lives of the Malays. Peletz contends that the coming of Islam did not displace the adat in the consciousness of the Malays but led to a selective syncretisation, which effectively linked the adat and Islam in such a manner as to preserve the entire realm of adat. This perspective is revealed clearly in several instances of his work. For instance, he asserts,

> we do know however that the animistic, partially Hinduised and matrilineally constituted Minangkabau of Sumatra had modified certain features of their adat pursuant both to the initial phases of their gradual and highly selective acceptance of Islamic beliefs and traditions and to their later efforts towards synthesizing additional elements of Islam with their historically altered culture and social system. But this is not to imply that Islam, which purports to offer its adherents an entirely self sufficient and sociologically perfected complex of behavioral ideals and institutions simply replaced long established adat practices and conceptions tied in with the social order or with human interactions with the powers of the supernatural. Indeed to take two examples, various aspects of Islamic jurisprudence and monotheism were not substituted for or somehow deemed to be mutually exclusive (because incompatible) with regard to centuries old moral, jural and religious

> conventions but were creatively interwoven with them in such a way as to preserve much of the integrity and holism characteristic of the pre-islamic adat (Peletz, 1981: 15).

Similarly, his construction of the Malays' understanding as embodied in the saying "*adat bersendi hukom, hukom bersendi kitabullah*" (Adat hinges on religious law, religion law hinges on the Book of God) is revealing of this perspective. Speaking for the Negri Malays, Peletz explains:

> far from being a conciliatory aphorism or platitude, as some would have it, this saying embodies a paramount cultural axiom of the type perhaps most appropriately classified as an "ultimate sacred proposition". Validated, reaffirmed and rendered sacrosanct through a variety of syncretic ritual performances and combining and symbolically harmonizing disparate elements of adat and Islam, this proposition not only guaranteed the integrity of the relationship between adat and Islam but also further sanctified the entire realm of adat by positing its inherent compatibility with Islamic religious law (Peletz, 1981: 17–18).

His selection of the "*kenduri* complex" as the classic example of the linkage between Islam and adat in the Malay mind and action is no less revealing of his presumption. Describing this ritual as one that is embedded in the adat social institution, he maintains that it comprises symbols both of Islam and adat, in which the worship of God is intermixed with ancestral offerings:

> Noteworthy here was the kenduri complex, an essential component of virtually all village rites and cooperative endeavors. The ritual complex typically entailed elaborate labor exchange, lavish hosting and feasting, sequences of Islamic prayers and chant, offerings of food and incense to local nature and ancestral spirits and the highly ceremonious presentation and joint consumption of areca nut embellished and wrapped in betel leaf—the latter being among the most powerful and accessible symbols of the property, morality, and permanence of the adat order (Peletz, 1981: 18–19).

He maintains that while Islamic orthodoxy admits no intermediaries between man and Allah, numerous conventions subsumed under the adat rubric, predicated on beliefs in Indic deities and pre-Hindu spiritual forces while containing specifically Islamic elements such as Quranic expressions, are diffused throughout the environment. According to Peletz, these conventions stress the necessity for the sake of the spiritual and material well-being of villages and the community's harmonious relationship with the domains of nature and the supernatural, of venerating ancestral culture heroes, guardian beings, and other local spirits as well as Allah (Peletz, 1981: 21).

Peletz's understanding of the religious orientation of the Malays is then used to explain the persistence of a system of land tenure and inheritance, which he perceives as conflicting with Islam. His views do not occur in a vacuum but are conditioned by the dominant perceptions on the subject. This stems from the notion articulated by colonial scholars that the syncretic character of the religious orientation of the Malays legitimizes and incorporates the pre-Islamic adat though these conflict with Islamic teachings. Given this perspective, Peletz presumes that the laws as practiced by the Malays of Rembau are contrary to Islam but are nevertheless upheld by them. Following his argument one can also be led to conclude that they consciously legitimise these practices as consistent with Islamic teachings although they acknowledge them to be distinct and of radically different origin. In this sense he perpetuates the basic flaw of his predecessors' unquestioning and uncritical acceptance of the adat-Islam conflict perspective in analyzing the Malay law of inheritance. This prevents him from perceiving the issue within the perspective of varying perceptions of Islamic law as understood by the Malays towards a system which originated from adat and which they deem compatible with Islam.

Peletz also touched upon the challenge posed to this once sacrosanct adat-Islam order by the phenomenon of rising Islamic consciousness amongst influential Muslim groups at the turn of the twentieth century, which he attributes strongly to colonial policies, among other factors. Peletz equates selected opinions on the law subscribed to by these groups as representative of the fact that adat law conflicts with Islam. Thus, he submits:

> among the most crucial historical points to be gleaned from the foregoing is that many of the villagers who have questioned or sought to break with the established adat order-whether in terms of the categorization and transmission of property, exogamy and marriage practices . . .—have justified their attitudes and actions by invoking precepts and standards drawn from and unambiguously associated with Islamic sources. This fact, in conjunction with parallel developments, testifies to the greatly expanded and ever increasing social relevance of Islam and more specifically to villagers' heightened assimilation of (if not more pronounced behavioral fidelity to) the canons of Islamic orthodoxy. Further, trends along these lines point to a broader ongoing process of relatively recent origin whereby the respective roles of adat

> and Islam are being reconceptualised, recast, and inverted, and the integrity of their interrelationship, once a sanctified given, is the subject of growing resentment. For the past decade or two, in marked contrast to the situation obtaining prior to the turn of the century and even up until independence in 1957, Islam, to a much greater extent than adat, has provided the symbols, imagery and standards with which villagers strive to orient their own behaviour and evaluate the actions of others . . . (Peletz, 1981: 45–46).

Peletz's analysis is misleading in so far as it equates ideas on Islam espoused by certain groups as with the case of the Religious Affairs Branch of the UMNO in 1951 as representative of Islam. His argument also implies that because these groups invoke or justify their beliefs utilizing Islamic sources, Islam as opposed to the adat is becoming increasingly relevant to their lives and they are more conscious of and have increasingly assimilated Islamic canons. Concluding that those who adhere to certain types of Islamic sources are more conscious of the canons of Islam and have increasingly assimilated these, is akin to declaring that these groups are more religious conscious as opposed to those who think otherwise. Such arguments are unacceptable, as a greater articulation of a certain brand of Islam does not make those who do not subscribe to it less religious or less appreciative of the relevance and significance of Islam to their lives. For instance, upholding Wahabbi interpretations of laws does not make one more Islamic conscious than not. The failure to perceive this distinction and the sole reliance on selected citations of "Islamic sources" as the only accurate representation of Islamic law on this aspect affects the accuracy of Peletz's claims.

Peletz's later work published in 1988 which also touches on this point, further attests to this flaw in reasoning. He disagreed with de Jong's analysis of the "adat crisis" of 1951 since according to him, it erroneously implied the existence of a cultural homogeneity of Negri Sembilan Malays. Rather, he ascribed to the view that the crisis reflected "conflicting cultural constructions of the relationship between the two institutions" between divergent groups in Negri Sembilan. Although on this we agree, his following argument pertaining to differential distribution of knowledge about Islam and its implications is subject to scrutiny.

Peletz subscribes to the view that there is a link between the "highly uneven distribution of knowledge pertaining to Islam" and the "shifting political fortunes of distinct groups of Malay leadership." This in turn influences perceptions of the relationship between adat and Islam on the question of inheritance. According to Peletz, it is essentially the rural Malays who view the relationship between adat and Islam largely in terms of complementarity while influential groups of Malay leadership, the products of rapid social change reinforced by colonial policies, perceive otherwise as they see incongruities between the two systems. Peletz maintains that the latter group is the more educated and highly literate members of the religious and political elite (Peletz, 1988: 121–25).

Peletz's argument strongly implies that those who view the adat as compatible with Islam are less steeped in knowledge pertaining to Islam. Presumably, if they are more knowledgeable in matters of Islam or more literate, they would see the incompatibility between the two systems. This also implies that not only the rural folks but the adat chiefs and all other Malays who disagree with such a point of view are less conscious of Islamic laws and teachings. The basic flaw in his argument is that it assumes the validity and theological correctness of certain opinions on inheritance law at the expense of others. This is misleading, as our arguments above have demonstrated. Thus, while Peletz dismisses de Jong's adat-Islam dichotomy as wanting, his arguments in fact reveal a similar paradigm. The cultural variations argument he propounds fails to account for an accurate understanding of the issue since it dismisses the possibility of different constructions of adat law based on Islam but posits the adat as distinct from Islam because groups or individuals who are part of a more educated class within the community are generally of the opinion that the adat laws relating to land and inheritance are unislamic. In this sense Peletz can be said to share the pitfall of the scholars of the past whom he had attempted to avoid.

The conflict perspective is also evident in numerous other writings, which we shall not examine here.[17] We have attempted to show that works on Malay land tenure and inheritance were influenced by the interests of colonial rule and colonial capitalism. We have also sought to "unmask" factors that may have conditioned the perception of the writers. Furthermore, attempts were also made to

[17] See, for instance, the thesis of Ismail bin Mat (1985: 84), who submits that "in practice many forms of adat laws which have prevailed in Malaysia since the introduction of Islamic law have also retained some of their customary elements that are in contradiction with the principles of Islamic law."

reveal some problems in their perceptions of these rules of adat, which affect a more comprehensive and accurate representation of the subject. These included a consistent attempt at portraying a conflict between the adat law and Islam and a superficial influence of Islam on the Malays particularly in the Adat Perpateh areas. So well entrenched is this perspective that it has influenced the views of post-colonial scholars thereby creating obstacles towards a more objective and accurate perception of Malay adat land laws.

CHAPTER FIVE

MALAY RULERS AND MALAY ADAT LAWS

Colonial writers on Malay adat laws never fail to point out that the laws buttress the autocratic power of the ruling class. Crawford, for instance, asserts that evidence of absolute government such as that found in other Indian nations is also contained in the laws of the Malays. He utilizes rules on language observed when addressing the monarch as a case in point. Comparing relevant Javanese laws to those of the Malays, Crawford submits:

> The language of the Malays and their laws contain similar evidence. To show the spirit of their instruction, I shall quote a few passages from their customary laws. The forbidden words are 'Titah', 'Berpatek', 'Murka', 'Ampun', 'Derma-Kurnia' and 'Anggurha'. If an inmate of the palace apply these terms to any but the prince, to whom they by right belong, he shall be put to death. If a person, without the walls use them, he shall be struck a blow over the mouth at the time he is pronouncing them. If any man, direct these words to be addressed to himself he shall suffer death.

Apart from these, Crawford also highlighted other laws in which he perceived "the same spirit is discernable." These included laws which prohibited the subjects, on pain of punishment, from assuming the privileges of the ruling class with respect to attire, the use of objects which are yellow and many others: "If persons come into the presence chamber, or even enter the precincts of the palace wearing clothes of extraordinary fineness, without the royal approbation, their clothes shall be torn from their backs and they shall be turned out." Furthermore, "if a person uses a mat for sleeping on, ornamented with yellow . . . or a yellow coloured pillow or a yellow handkerchief, the punishment of such offence is death." Similarly, 'if a person wears a golden titled kris without the royal order, such a kris shall be taken from him and confiscated'" (Crawford, 1967: 17).

The perception that adat sanctioned autocratic rule continued to pervade the thinking of subsequent writers such as Wilkinson and Winstedt. However, these authors confined such evaluation to the

Adat Temenggong. Wilkinson, for instance, claimed that the adat comprised legislation "drawn up for the glorification of the court" (Hooker, 1970: 34).

Wilkinson further suggested that the privileges and might of the ruling class sanctioned by the adat can be understood in relation to the immense significance of the ruler's position in the society. According to him, the ruler in traditional Malay society was of divine authority:

> A Malay Raja was personally sacred. He was believed to heal diseases with his touch, he might perform miracles, and he was considered almost invulnerable. He was immeasurably above his subjects, who were only permitted to address themselves to the dust beneath his feet. He was the source of all honour and the fountain of all justice. In Moslem times he styled himself a Sultan, a Caliph, a Commander of the Faithful, a Shadow of God upon Earth. Any insult or indignity to a prince was a sacrilege; it exposed the perpetrator to all kinds of spiritual punishments. Even to roughly handle a king's regalia was a deadly offence. If a commoner assumed the air or attributes of a prince, if he wore the royal yellow or flew the royal flag, he was believed to expose himself to certain death at the hands of ghostly protectors of royal dignities. The commoner had no rights whatever; the king could do whatever seemed best in his own eyes. Such at least, was the theory of Malay government (Hooker, 1970: 35).

Instances from the records on Malay history were utilized to support their proposition. Many of these were used to reveal the apparent unconditional rights of Malay rulers (Hooker, 1970: 36–38).

The writers further assumed that Islam was a contributory factor to the development of despotism. Crawford, for instance, reveals this perception in his attempts to explain the source of autocratic rule of Malay governments. Islam is viewed as one of the decisive factors which sanctioned unlimited authority and power of the rulers, as the following remarks illustrate: "No doubt the arbitrary maxims imported along with the Mohammadan and Hindu religions have contributed . . . to the establishment of uncontrolled despotism among the tribes" (Crawford, 1967: 11). The perception is further reinforced in his assessment of the nature of rule in neighbouring countries such as Macassar: "It was this, that on the introduction of the Mohammadan religion among the Macassars, a succession of able princes with the influence acquired by their extensive conquests seem to have put them in the way of becoming absolute" (Crawford, 1967: 24).

That such a perception persisted even after a century or so is evident in the study of Wilkinson. His appraisal of the Adat Temenggong furnishes evidence of this. Wilkinson distinguished the Adat Temenggong from the Adat Perpateh on the ground that the Adat Temenggong was influenced by Islam and Hinduism. He was also of the opinion that the Adat Temenggong was despotic and autocratic. By implication, Wilkinson believed that Islam contributed to these negative traits of the adat (Hooker, 1970: 32). Hooker also implies a similar perception when he remarked that the tendencies in the Malay digests to give prominence to the sultan similar to the tendency found in the Hindu codes "have been given greater impetus with the introduction of Islam, which may have tended to invest the ruler with functions unknown to traditional law" (Hooker, 1968: 166).

The writers also suggest that it was the English who first introduced egalitarian conceptions of law in the Malay states. This position is amply conveyed in Wilkinson's evaluative comparison of the law prior to the influence of British rule, with the effects of those introduced by the colonial power, as the following remarks convey: "The adat Temenggong is made up of ordinary Malay custom, administered by despotic authority and supplemented by a large number of sumptuary regulations drawn up for the glorification of the court. The latter feature appealed very much to the old Malays. . . ." (Hooker, 1970: 34). Contextually, the term "old Malays" can only refer to those who were never subjected to the influence of British law. Wilkinson further reinforces this position by juxtaposing his evaluation with Abdullah Munshi's criticism against the feudal custom of kings in Terengganu. Abdullah, as we know, lived in Singapore and Malacca under direct British administration. Through the perceptions of Abdullah, who by implication represented the "new Malay", Wilkinson sought to show that it was the influence of the English, which effectively challenged the class bias in Malay adat laws.

Yet another indication of such a perception is evident in Wilkinson's view that it was English law, which checked the unrestrained power of Malay rulers towards their subjects. As the author himself remarks: "Under the circumstances, it is not difficult to paint a very highly coloured picture of the immense improvement in the position of the Malay ryot since the introduction of British rule" (Hooker, 1970: 35).

These views also recur in the writings of Winstedt (1953: 96) who maintains that "in no sphere has British influence been more beneficial than in the sphere of law." He believed that English law was characterized by fairness and equality. Thus he asserts: "Universal validity, impartiality and comparative humanity distinguish British justice and only one Malay system of law can challenge any comparison" (Winstedt, 1953: 98). This system of law was none other than the Adat Perpateh, which Winstedt perceived as uninfluenced by Islam and other foreign elements.

The author's portrayal of the stark inequalities and the autocratic traits of Malay laws are doubtless on record. They mirror and institutionalize the Malay feudal social order and its corresponding system of values. In the rigidly hierarchical society in which distinctions in rank and power are greatly emphasized, such laws served to maintain the status and might of the Malay ruling class at the expense of the Malay subjects.[1] Furthermore, by constantly reinforcing social inequalities, the laws affected the development of despotism. As Shaharuddin Maaruf, in a study on Malay feudal values, aptly submits: "When ideas of hierarchy, inequality, superiority and inferiority are constantly impressed upon the mind, it is bound to have far-reaching effects on the development of personality and character. Culture and ethics assume the authoritarian forms with its strong sadistic and masochistic traits. On the one hand we have a lack of restraint among the ruling class and on the other, servility and submission amongst the subject class" (Maaruf, 1981: 8).

Our disagreement, however, lies with the writers' fallacious notion that Islam is partly responsible for the absolute and despotic power of Malay rulers sanctioned by the adat. On the contrary, long before the advent of European power and its influence in the sphere of law, legal reformist ideas introduced by Islam had checked the unconditioned and arbitrary power of Malay rulers. Islam introduced the idea of the rule of law by which the exercise of the rulers' power was subject to law and the subjects granted rights such that they would not be made to suffer the arbitrary will of the rulers. Even though Malay rulers were hardly, if ever, punished for violating these principles of rule, nevertheless, it is pertinent to note that the reformist legal thought brought by Islam succeeded in permeating the consciousness of the Malay ruling class who accepted and maintained them as ideal standards of rule. This holds true in spite of the fact that Malay rulers often flouted and transgressed the injunctions determined by Islam. Support for our contention is found in the instances

[1] For an analysis of Malay feudal society and its corresponding system of values, please see S.H. Alatas (1972), Shaharuddin Maaruf (1981) Chapter 1.

recorded in Malay historical sources. They reveal the grossly erroneous perception of the writers that Islam contributed to the development of despotic laws. On the contrary, without the elements of restraint introduced by Islam, the ethics and conduct of Malay rulers would have been even worse.

One of the most instructive sources which reveals the restraining impact of Islam upon the exercise of the power of the Malay ruling class is the *Sejarah Melayu* (*Malay Annals*). It constitutes perhaps the most comprehensive record of sixteenth century Malay society and its feudal customs. The authoritative value of the *Annals* is supported by the fact that the ruler himself commissioned it to be written as a record of the stories, ethics and customs of Malay rulers for the benefit of future descendants (Shellabear, 1967: 3). It therefore provides the best source of evidence which conveys the rights and limitations of the ruling class *vis-a-vis* their subjects. The *Annals* is significant for yet another reason. It is also the text selectively utilized by writers such as Wilkinson to portray the unlimited power of Malay rulers. Yet it is this source, which is saturated with rules limiting their power, which bears the unmistakable influence of Islam.[2]

Take, for instance, Wilkinson's example of the ruler's complicity to murder, an account which the author utilizes to show the unlimited power of rulers under the Adat Temenggong (Hooker, 1970: 37–38). This event is undeniably on record. The ruler in question was Sultan Mahmud. The *Annals* reveal that this very sultan knew and accepted the limitations of his power by law, which were invariably established by Islam. One wonders at the unrestrained power, which the rulers would otherwise have exercised if it had not been for these limitations. A classic instance occurred when the sultan was caught by Tun Biajid leaving the latter's house one day at dawn. Tun Biajid was returning home from duty. Angrily he rebuked the sultan: "Is this how you treat me. It is a pity that you are my master. If you were not, I would not be a man if I did not spear you!" The sultan's reaction as he held his men back from attacking Tun Biajid is extremely pertinent. It reveals an awareness and acceptance of the sanctions imposed by Islam upon the arbitrary abuse of power.

[2] On the Islamic conception of kingship, please refer to Al-Ghazali (1961). For the Malay version, please refer to Hussain (1966). For an application of the Islamic conception of leadership to Malay society, please see Alatas (1972), and Maaruf (1984).

"He speaks the truth, I have been wrong to him. According to the law (*hukum*), he ought to kill me, but because he is a Malay subject and does not wish to commit treason, he restrained himself" (Shellabear, 1967: 186).

The incident instructively reveals the egalitarian traits of Islamic precepts, which were understood by the Malay ruling class prior to the influence of English law. The ruler himself acknowledged that he was not above the law and should not be spared of his wrong-doing and that his retribution was not inconsistent with his position as a Malay ruler. Although Sultan Mahmud was ultimately saved on the ground of a feudal custom that a subject must never commit treason, the incident is pertinent in revealing that Islam, as far back as the sixteenth century, had challenged the absolute power of Malay rulers.

When Malay rulers exercised restraints in the use of their power, this could only be attributed to the influence of the principles of Islam. Again, the conduct of Sultan Mahmud reveals this point. When the sultan came to study Sufism (Islamic mysticism), accompanied by a large number of his retainers, the *maulana* (religious master) rudely refused him, saying: "why should a sultan visit the house of a *fakir* (poor)?" Significantly enough, the sultan, who would have put to death even those who did him no wrong, accepted the *fakir*'s impolite rejection, only to return again during the night, carrying his own *kitab* (religious book) and accompanied by only two of his men. The sultan even addressed himself as "*fakir* Mahmud" (Shellabear, 1967: 195–96). The point the Maulana was trying to convey to the sultan is evident. It is that even a ruler is a servant of God, and that his power and wealth do not determine his greatness or honour. The sultan himself understood this principle and accepted it.

Even if in some cases, the influence of Islam in curbing the rulers' uncontained lust for power, wealth and position is received in extreme ways, they nevertheless reveal that Malay rulers under the influence of Islam accepted the performance of acts of piety as superior to unlimited power and prestige. The *Annals* reveals how rulers completely abandoned their thrones in order to devote themselves to missionary activity. The case of Sultan Muhammad Shah serves as an example. We are told that when a ship arrived in his land to spread Islam to neighbouring countries, the king appointed his son as the ruler. He himself abdicated his position, donned the robe of a *fakir* and left his country to propagate Islam (Shellabear, 1967: 53).

Apart from imposing checks and restraints upon the ruler's power, the influence of Islam also extends to defining clearly the rights of Malay subjects against the arbitrary abuse of power by Malay rulers. Rulers who acted despotically in practice did so without the support of theoretical precepts, which limited their power. The conditions upon which Malay subjects pledged their loyalty and subservience to rulers, as witnessed by the agreement between Demang Lebar Daun and Sang Sapurba, respectively, is a case in point.

The ruler must not mistreat his subjects nor can he punish them arbitrarily except when they transgress God's law. In the words of Demang Lebar Daun, "the descendants of your humble servant shall be the subject of your Majesty's throne, but they must be well treated by your descendants. If they offend, they shall not, however grave their offence, be humiliated or reviled with evil words; if their offence is grave let them be put to death, if that is in accordance with God's law" (Shellabear, 1967: 25). Though it is undeniable that the condition of unquestioning loyalty by the subjects required in exchange for the ruler's patronage and protection is unislamic, nevertheless the agreement does reveal that restraints on arbitrary or cruel treatment by rulers of their subjects is invariably imposed by Islam.

Long before the introduction of English law, Islam had already taught Malay rulers that they must respect the rule of the law, govern judiciously and avoid oppression and injustice. Perhaps one of the best sources of evidence of the fundamental idea that Malay rulers acknowledged that they were not above the law in the exercise of their power is found in the rulers' deathbed testaments. Though Malay rulers seldom lived according to these prescribed rules, their deathbed counsel to surviving heirs remain extremely pertinent precisely because they were made at the point of death. Given the critical circumstances in which they were uttered, it is not unreasonable to maintain that Malay rulers accepted these principles of law, which were undoubtedly Islamic. The deathbed counsel of Sultan Malikut Tahir is a case in point. The sultan was guilty of cruelty and abuse of power. He had had his brother kidnapped because the latter had taken away one of the ladies at his court and ordered the execution of his brother's retainer as a result of this incident (Shellabear, 1967: 62–63). Yet, when confronted with death, the ruler's advice to his son reveals an awareness that he had rashly and wrongfully transgressed the boundaries of law which Islam established: "My beloved son, . . . exercise a great deal of patience towards all wrongdoers, do not take lightly your worship towards God Most High and do not unjustly take away the rights of others" (Shellabear, 1967: 65).

Yet another instance of the ruler's acknowledgement of the rule of law long established by Islam is also revealed in the deathbed counsel of Melaka's Sultan Mansur Shah. When faced with death, the ruler exhorted his son to observe propriety and justice in the exercise of his power. His counsel also shows that Islam grants Malay subjects the right to seek redress if justice is denied them:

> Know, my dear son that this world is impermanent . . . Only a sound faith and good conduct is eternal. After I am gone, my son, you should practise patience and justice and do not be greedy over the property of others because living off the property of fellow Muslims is indeed a great sin, unpardonable by God. Do not turn away from those who come before you because every one of God's servants is your responsibility. Help them if they are in difficulty. If they are victimised, you should investigate the matter very carefully so that you will not be burdened . . . in the Hereafter . . . your just intervention will be enquired into. God will ask the subjects about their rulers . . . therefore you should enforce justice and equality so that God will lighten your account (Shellabear, 1967: 164–65).

Sultan Maliku's Saleh's testament also shares the same spirit. It reveals that Islam taught Malay rulers that they were not above the law and should thus not encroach upon the lawful rights of others: "My dear sons, do not be greedy for the property of others; do not desire wives of men and daughters of your servants . . . avoid that which is improper . . ." (Shellabear, 1967: 57).

Impartiality in dispensing judgment and compliance with Islamic commands also constitutes some of the constraints, which Islam imposes upon rulers. They reveal that Islam could not have contributed to the development of authoritarian and capricious rule. The deathbed advice of Bendahara Paduka Raja to Sultan Mahmud clearly illustrates this point: "Do not listen to the words of those who are untrue. If you comply, you will regret your action. Contain your desires for they are the work of the devil. Allah has destroyed many a great king because they have chosen to follow the path of their desires and emotions (Shellabear, 1967: 184). Though formal punishment for the rulers' transgression of law was inconceivable in Malay feudal society, nevertheless the *Annals* records strong evidence that Malay rulers acknowledged that they were subject to divine retribution for their wrongdoings. This troubled their conscience in a positive way. Some of the questions that preoccupied the rulers implied a constant and excessive fear of the extent and duration of punishment for wrongs done on earth. This is brought to light in the answer which Sultan Mansur Shah wished to hear from the religious teachers in Pasai. The question he forwarded was: "Will the inhabitants of heaven be forever in heaven, will the inhabitants of hell remain forever in hell?". Though ultimately the answer given pleased the sultan, the incident reveals nonetheless that Islam was a contending force against arbitrary power. Without the influence of Islam, the condition may have been even worse (Shellabear, 1967: 150–53).

Apart from the *Malay Annals*, the influence of Islam in imposing limits on the power of Malay rulers and regulating its use towards just ends is also evident in the historical records of neighbouring kingdoms. Recourse to such sources is pertinent since the attempts by colonial writers such as Wilkinson to appraise the Adat Temenggong extended beyond the confines of the Malay Peninsula (Hooker, 1970: 31). These records further reveal the unfounded claim of adat law writers that Islam was a contributory factor to autocratic laws.

Take, for instance, the *Bustan al-Salatin*, a seventeenth century composition in the Malay language concerning the "actions and deeds of kings of former times and later." The author, Nur al-Din al-Raniri, was commissioned to write the book by the sultan of Acheh himself, Iskandar Thani. The book contained humanitarian principles of government based upon conceptions of kingship in Islam. The fact that the ruler himself authorized the work clearly indicates that they accepted and ascribed importance to Islamic injunctions, which circumscribed and regulated their power.

The text is instructive in revealing that by virtue of the influence of Islam, Malay rulers acknowledged that they were not empowered to legislate arbitrarily. On the contrary, laws they promulgated had to be subjected to the authority established in the *hadith* and the Quran, which served as limitations to the unbounded exercise of legislative power. Instances of such laws expounded by the rulers included those which institutionalized charity through *zakat*, a taxation for the improvement of the welfare of the people, the abolition of gambling and cockfighting, and the eradication of laws which were arbitrary and cruel, such as trial by ordeal. In the administration of justice, rulers were also bound to ensure that Malay subjects who were victimized arbitrarily could obtain rights of redress (Iskandar, 1966: 32–45).

Even if it is argued that these instances were historically doubtful and that the text was commissioned as an ideological justification for the ruling class, the fact remains that with the influence of Islam, Malay rulers were obliged to legitimize their rule by appealing to these principles of rule. In this way, they avoided giving their legislation the appearance of arbitrariness.

Apart from this, the *Bustan al-Salatin* also contains many parables which clearly reveal that Islam had taught Malay rulers to observe moderation and restraint in the exercise of their powers. The parables vividly convey tales of divine retribution, which befell rulers who deviated from Islamic laws governing kings. They scorned rulers who were preoccupied with excessive wealth and power and emphasized the honour credited to those who led simple lives, who gave alms to the poor even if they had nothing to spare for themselves, who treated their subjects justly (Grinter, 1975). In this way these parables served as counsel to rulers to avoid abusing their position and power.

Yet another pertinent source which reveals that Islam had long curbed the arbitrary exercise of power of Malay rulers, is evident in the *Tuhfat al Nafis* (*The Precious Gift*).[3] The book comprises tales and stories about Malay kings and their Bugis allies. Had adat law writers taken into consideration this source, they would have realized that Islamic principles of just rule had penetrated the consciousness of Malay rulers and defined the limits of their authority. For instance, the *Tuhfat* describes with disgust the conduct of Sultan Mahmud, who constantly defied and flouted Islamic tenets. He was preoccupied only with idle amusements. His conduct was not oriented towards improving the welfare of his subjects. Instead, one of his favorite pastimes was to take pleasure trips to neighbouring countries, where he patronized what the author of the *Tuhfat* referred to as "unsuitable places." The sultan also kept a bunch of idle young retainers who were irresponsible troublemakers. Furthermore, the sultan was always intent upon following his own desires (Raja Ali, 1965: 338–40).

[3] The *Tuhfat* was written by Raja Ali Haji, a member of the royal family at Riau. His father, Raja Ahmad, was the son of the famous Bugis hero Raja Haji. Raja Ali Haji himself was an important figure in Riau's administration. The *Tuhfat* gives an account of nearly two centuries of events that occurred in the Malay kingdom and traces the relationship between Malay and Bugis kings. To date, no author has challenged the reliability of this book.

Sultan Mahmud's conduct was never approved by the majority of the ruling class. In fact, rulers repeatedly attempted to reform him. This clearly implied that, contrary to the conception of writers such as Wilkinson; Malay rulers could not do whatever they pleased. Even if they misbehaved, their misdemeanours reflected a deviation from established customs and the tradition shaped by Islam. This was in fact the reasoning maintained by the author of the *Tuhfat*: "I need say no more. Sultan Mahmud was a young man and those who accompanied him were young servants and attendants who could diminish the kingdom's prestige because they were ill-versed in the traditional customs" (Raja Ali, 1965: 339). Interpreted in its context, "traditional customs" could only mean Islamic ones. This construction is supported by the fact that the *Tuhfat* consistently upheld rulers who were portrayed as complying with the precepts of Islam (Raja Ali, 1965: 346–48).

The above examples derived from Malay historical sources are pertinent and instructive. They reveal that even before colonial rule, Islam had strongly contended against the unfettered power of Malay rulers. It introduced the principle of the rule of law and established that rulers like their subjects, are bound by law, irrespective of their status in society. Islam also defined Malay rulers' duties and liabilities towards their subjects in no uncertain terms. It further allowed the subjects rights, which the ruler must ensure. In failing to take into consideration this pertinent point, the writers reveal their lack of knowledge of Malay legal history.

The erroneous allegation that Islam was a contributory factor to the development of despotic laws may have stemmed from the writers' inability to distinguish the Islamic from the feudal elements of the law. The failure to perceive this essential difference is a serious shortcoming in the conceptualization of Malay adat laws. Wilkinson portrays such an erroneous perception. His remark that "even using the wrong kind of clothing and beating of gongs at weddings are severely punished under the Mohammadan law," supports this view (Hooker, 1970: 10). Wilkinson was most probably referring to rules which prohibited the Malay subjects from using certain colours and kinds of attire worn by the rulers, which were their sole prerogative. These constitute part of the numerous laws, which served to preserve and entrench the authority of the ruling class contrary to the spirit and teachings of Islam. In Islam, social equality is emphasized.

Islam teaches that a leader should not succumb to snobbery or express social distance between himself and his people. Thus Caliph Ali, in his instruction to Malik al-Ashtar, Governor of Egypt, succinctly remarked:

> You must take care not to cut yourself off from the people. Do not place a curtain of false prestige between you and those over whom you rule. Such protection and show of pomp and pride are in reality manifestations of inferiority complex and vanity. The result of such an attitude is that you remain ignorant of the condition of your subjects and of the actual causes of events occurring in the state (Jafri, 1984: 642–43; Maaruf, 1984: 9–11).

Such evidence also proves erroneous Hooker's assertion that Islam "provided no epistemological or religious reason" to alter rules in the Malay digests which prescribe outward trappings of rank, elements which he perceived as based upon Hindu caste values (Hooker, 1968: 170).

Yet another indication of the failure to perceive a distinction between Islam and legal elements which supported the feudal social order is strongly implied in Wilkinson's attempt to weave the divine conception of kingship into the concept of the ruler being God's representative on earth. Portraying the view that in traditional Malay society, the ruler is conceived as a divine authority, Wilkinson continues: "In Moslem times, he styled himself Sultan, Caliph, Commander of the Faithful, Shadow of God on Earth. Any insult or indignity to the prince was a sacrilege, it exposed the perpetrator to all kinds of spiritual punishment" (Hooker, 1970: 35).

Such an assertion, it can be argued, implied that Islam further entrenched the concept of divine kingship. However, this conception is misleading. It is invoked to justify and legitimize the power of the ruler in ways that are inconsistent with the teachings of Islam. As one author aptly remarks ". . . this theory of kingship is not a faithful representation of the Islamic doctrine. It is precisely the use or abuse of religious ideas that give force to the whole conception of the divinity of kings" (Maznah, 1985: 68).

This conception portrays the ruler as possessing magical character and origin and hence hereditary right to office. It also serves as an ideological tool to ensure complete submission and obedience to the ruler's authority. Such a notion does not accord with Islam. Several relevant aspects of kingship defined in Islam that oppose the above are as follows: (a) Sovereignty belongs to God and not to the state or the rulers. (b) Those in authority are to be selected from among the members of the community on the ground that they are capable and trustworthy. (c) They should enjoin good and forbid evil. (d) The noblest amongst them is the most righteous and pious. (e) The best leaders are those who love the people and are in turn loved by them. (f) The affairs of government are not to be assigned to those who are out for positions moved by their greed for them. (g) Obedience to the ruler is obligatory as long as it does not entail violation of the Islamic commands. There is no obedience in sin but only in virtue. (h) Anyone in a position of authority, even if he is a slave, must be obeyed as long as he enjoins good and forbids evil. (i) The rulers must not legislate against what is already laid down in the Quran and the Tradition of the Prophet which belongs to the eternal principles of Islam. (j) The ruler should defend and honour the property, the life and the dignity of all his subjects irrespective of class or creed. (k) Everyone in authority including the Caliph is not above the law. If the Caliph commits a transgression he is to be judged by law, to which even the Prophet himself was subordinated (Alatas, 1965: 119–20).

A pertinent study which reveals clarity in identifying the actual sources of laws that promote despotism and class interest is accomplished by Abdullah Munshi in his book *Kisah Pelayaran Abdullah*. This work is directly relevant in illustrating the erroneous perception of the writers that Islam contributed to the autocratic and in-egalitarian traits of Malay laws. Abdullah's work was accessible to colonial adat law writers. In fact Wilkinson, even relied upon Abdullah to support his view that the Adat Temenggong is despotic. Yet Wilkinson failed to pay adequate attention to Abdullah's consistent attempts at discerning the source of ills of Malay laws.

Abdullah's reasoning and arguments clearly show that he was critical of laws that entrenched the Malay feudal social structure and its corresponding values, showing that these were not the result of Islamic influence. In Pahang, for example, he described the custom that allowed criminals and murderers to escape punishment by simply seeking the king's pardon and enslaving themselves to his service. These men could do anything they pleased; they even stirred trouble without being punished since they received the sultan's protection. Furthermore, if one ruler's *hamba raja* (as they were called) was killed, a compensation of seven men was demanded in return (Abdullah Munshi, 1981: 14–15). The effect of this custom, according to Abdullah, brought injustice to the people. Similarly, when he was in Terengganu, Abdullah further criticized rules which institutionalized inequalities between the ruler and his subject. When he asked the officer what were the laws of the land, he was told that he should not use an umbrella on the king's ground, that he could not put on shoes or clothes that were yellow, nor could he carry weapons. Abdullah smiled at what he regarded as the "folly and pettiness of the laws" (Abdullah Munshi, 1981: 21). He also mentioned other customary practices such as those that allowed rulers to take away wives and daughters of their subjects (Abdullah Munshi, 1981: 24). In Kelantan, Abdullah learnt of the accustomed right of rulers to forced labour. The Malay masses were expected to engage in the services of the Raja indefinitely, while both they and their families fended for themselves without maintenance by the rulers (Abdullah Munshi, 1981: 55).

However, Abdullah did not perceive these despotic customs as due to the influence of Islam. In fact, he explicitly attacked these laws upon Islamic grounds. His argument against the trivialities of the law clearly reveals this:

> Does it mean that a ruler is degraded or humiliated when a visitor puts on yellow attire or uses an umbrella merely because he wants shelter from the sun. It is as though the kings seek honour and greatness from externalities and trivialities, not from the goodness of his heart and his sense of justice.... If the ruler is a virtuous one, he ought to guard against being despised and show concern for the welfare of the people and institutionalize just laws so that people are protected against oppression, misfortune and poverty.... Is it not right that a ruler issues punishment on matters only because they are sinful? As such, he must never execute punishment on matters which do not sin against God or which do not undermine the ruler's authority or do not constitute wrong towards mankind.

Abdullah also suggested alternative examples of those laws he perceived to be socially beneficial. All these are Islamic in spirit and content. For instance, he questioned why there were no laws against opium smoking despite the fact that it ruined one's health; he similarly wondered about the absence of laws against gambling or laws which prohibited the use of filthy and smelly attire, or those which prevented people from doing as they pleased or from being indolent or irresponsible or disrespectful, or from living in dirt and filth (Abdullah Munshi, 1981: 21–23).[4]

Abdullah's counsel to Tengku Temarau while he was in Kelantan is yet another instructive indication that he, unlike writers on adat, perceived the source of despotism and inequality in Malay laws. His counsel to the Malay ruler is couched upon Islamic precepts, which he offered as alternatives to the injustice of Malay feudal laws and customs:

> Remember Tengku, that you will be questioned by God in the Hereafter on the affairs of your subjects . . . those who will be the first to enter Hell are rulers who are unjust to their subjects and the first to be rewarded are those who do justice to them. . . . Do not think that those who become kings are greater and more honoured than their subjects because even the king is a servant of God. When one is appointed by God as ruler, it is not to satisfy his desire, to have ten or twenty wives or to plunder and kill oppressively unless commanded by God, as a protection for mankind so that there will be no oppression of one man by another. As such, it is essential that all rulers devote themselves to the study of *Taj al-Salatin* (*Crown of Kings*) each day and that they seek learned men to teach and advise them so that they will know the stories of rulers who are just and those who are unjust" (Abdullah Munshi, 1981: 73).[5]

In a way, Abdullah's critique represents an extension of the tradition based upon Islam, which contended against the un-circumscribed power of the ruling class recorded as far back as the sixteenth century.

Apart from his ability to grasp accurately the source of the ills of Malay laws as compared to the colonial adat law writers, Abdullah's work also serves well in illustrating their lack of objectivity in evaluating the adat. Unlike these writers, Abdullah did not undermine the entire legal sources of the Malays. While he severely criticized

---

[4] One of the most important values enjoined by Islam is the respect for life (Sv: Verse35). Opium smoking, which ruins life, is certainly contrary to Islamic teachings. Islam also condemns gambling (Sii: Verse 219) and scorns irresponsibility (Svi: Verse 164). The Qur'an emphasises that man is accountable for all his actions. Furthermore, personal cleanliness is regarded as so important in Islam that even the Qur'an draws upon the virtues and methods of personal hygiene (Sv: Verse 7).

[5] The Taju Salatin is a comprehensive code on kingship and the law based upon the doctrine of Islam. It defines the fundamental principles of government, determines the limits of the powers of the ruling class and their obligations towards their subjects. The book was believed to have been translated into Malay in Acheh sometime in the 17th century.

and called for the eradication of those laws that served the interests of the ruling class at the expense of the subject class, he never failed to highlight the benefits of useful sources of laws which would positively reform Malay society. Abdullah advocated this in spite of the fact that he admired tremendously the virtues of aspects of English law, which he duly credited (Abdullah Munshi, 1981: 88–91).

It is also pertinent to point out that, just as some Malay rulers arbitrarily abused their power in violation of the law sanctioned by Islam, British colonial masters were similarly guilty of disrespect for the rule of law, causing suffering to their native subjects. But this by itself does not mean that English law is despotic, in the way that Islam cannot be blamed for the autocratic exercise of power of Malay rulers. A classic example is recorded by Abdullah in his *Hikayat*. The matter concerned the conduct of a certain senior officer by the name of Mr. Bean who served at Colonel Farquhar's Residence in Malacca. This officer's action was certainly unlawful. According to Abdullah,

> Mr. Bean was an ill-natured man with a very bad temper. He put two soldiers on guard at the door of his house and children of any race who passed by along the road he caught and put into a fenced compound, the gate being shut on them. If the children ran away too fast to be caught, they were pursued by two dogs and in the ensuing scramble they would be caught and shut up. When he had collected many children, Mr. Bean brought them out in pairs and made them box each other. Any child unwilling to box he ordered to be caned, so for fear of this they boxed. He had to take great delight in this, leaping about and roaring with laughter. The young boxers had bruised faces and noses. He noted anyone who was bloodied and gave him more money than those who were not before he let them go. Then he would call another pair. He spent every day thus watching human blood flowing... Nobody had the courage to stop Mr. Bean but it aroused the hatred and fear of all the best people who dared not allow children to pass along that road. After a short while, Mr. Bean did not want children anymore but took adults instead and made them box....

In spite of all his gross abuse and causing men and children physical and psychological pain, Mr. Bean never suffered punishment. As Abdullah remarked, "I was surprised that Mr. Farquhar who became Resident of Malacca at the time took no action over the doings of his officer for other races despised the things I have mentioned which they held to be typical of the behaviour of all Englishmen, following the Malay proverb, 'a single buffalo had mud on it and the whole herd is smeared'" (Abdullah Munshi, 1985: 72–73).

Abdullah's account of the behaviour of all Englishmen in Malacca further illustrates the lawlessness present in the colonial ruling class as among the native ruling class. For example, he noted that people looked upon Englishmen as tigers because of their misbehaviour and aggressiveness. Drunken English sailors smashed in the doors of houses, robbed and looted the property of stallholders in the market and caused much disturbance. Even slaves, not to speak of women and children, could not walk about in the streets for fear of being assaulted (Abdullah Munshi, 1985: 72; Alatas, 1977: 132–34).

Furthermore, while colonial writers selected and criticized the privileges of the Malay ruling class that the law sanctioned, they remained silent with respect to colonial policies which reinforced and entrenched the status and advantages enjoyed by the Malay ruling class. Such policies were not criticized because they served the interest of the colonial power. For example, under colonial rule, the Malay ruling class was guaranteed a large, stable income, which was promptly paid. Hitherto, such an advantage was never enjoyed by Malay rulers. Even the palaces in which they lived after the advent of colonialism were known to have been more splendid than those that had been their lot before. Malay members of the ruling class were also ensured security and an increase in their position and prestige, an advantage they did not have in the past. In addition, the British had always encouraged Malay rulers to engage in private business ventures (Emerson, 1964: 140; Alatas, 1972: 97). By appeasing traditional Malay rulers and their chief's with these privileges the colonial power minimized dissatisfaction and ensured a smooth running of their administration.

Furthermore, colonial adat law writers made no objections to the policy (which perpetuated authoritarian rule) suggested before the Federal Council in 1927, in which the prominent British Resident Hugh Clifford was known to have submitted the following:

> These states [i.e., the Federated Malay States] were, when the British government was invited by their rulers and chiefs to set their troubled houses in order, Mohammedan monarchies. Such as they are today, and such they must continue to be. No mandate has ever been extended by Rajas, chiefs or people to vary the system of government which had existed in these territories from time immemorial: and in these

> days, when democratic and socialist theories and doctrine are spreading like an infection, bringing with them too often, not peace but a sword, I feel it incumbent upon me to emphasize the utter inapplicability of any form of democratic or popular government to the circumstances of FMS, the system must in its essence be autocratical.[6]

Attempts by colonial writers such as Winstedt at an evaluative comparison of adat and English law upon the basis of equality and universality are also marred by the one-sided portrayal of English law. For instance, Winstedt, like Wilkinson, challenged Malay adat laws on the grounds that it promoted class favouritism. Crawford's attempt at portraying the inequalities in punishment depending upon the status of the victim, as instructive of the spirit of the law, is yet another instance. Contextually, Crawford (1967: 112) implies that, by contrast, the laws of the English are free from the taint of inequality.

These assertions are naive and do not provide a balanced portrayal of the law. There are also many instances in the history of English law, which reveal a great deal of inequalities the authors completely overlooked. Many of these favoured the rich at the expense of the working class. For instance, between 1750 and 1850 in England, the condition of the working class was appalling. Both the law and its administrators were not absolved from this. In factories for instance, a system of fines was imposed which enabled owners to exploit the workers. So oppressive was the system that even if a worker fell ill, and could not find a substitute, he had to pay for the steam "unnecessarily produced" which might be as much as half his weekly wage. This condition illustrates factory legislation at the time (Kuczynski, 1942: 21).

Even legislation passed by parliament failed to serve as effective checks on the abuse of the workers, due to the administrators of the law who had a personal interest in preventing its implementation. This occurred in the case of the truck system. The system compelled workers to buy food in company controlled stores at prices above normal. Like the fine system, it was held by employers to get back as much as possible the wages of workers. There were a number of pieces of legislation forbidding the system but they were not enforced. Employers simply declined to obey the law. The magistrates either could not compel them or they themselves were the employers or had friends and relatives who were employers.

[6] Proceedings, Nov. 16, 1927.

The Vagrancy Acts further weakened and oppressed the poor. Those who attempted to enforce the law either by means of strikes or by compelling employers to observe them were imprisoned, flogged or transported to penal settlements abroad. Even the children of the poor were not spared the inequalities of the law. William Pitt, Prime Minister around the turn of the nineteenth century, proposed in his Poor Law Bill that children especially those in textile industries, should start work at the age of five. In factories and mines, children worked for twelve hours or even more. Often they slept in the factories or fell asleep beside machines during working hours resulting in innumerable incidents. Furthermore, at the turn of the nineteenth century, what was called "Combination Laws" was passed to safeguard employers against the strikes and unrest of the working classes. In effect, the laws allowed owners of mills unlimited freedom to impose working and living conditions upon the workers (Kuczynski, 1942: 21–35).[7]

Colonial adat law writers could not have been unaware of the legal shortcomings affecting the working classes in their own societies. Yet, they ignored these problems in their evaluative comparison of English law with Malay adat laws. As such, their comparison is neither an objective nor an accurate representation of the law.

[7] For an account of earlier legislation in England to the same effect, please refer to R.H. Tawney (1960: 253–73).

CONCLUSION

This thesis has examined pertinent studies on Malay adat laws by several prominent colonial writers and some continuities. The aim has not been not to provide an alternative account of the laws. Instead, the focus has been an analysis of the authors' approach, conceptualization and evaluation of the subject.

A portrayal of their essential ideas and judgment was the thrust of Chapter One. Generally, writers conceived Malay adat laws as being primitive, backward, inhumane, unequal, and ineffective in ensuring the security of life and property. Raffles even went so far as to assert that the laws were primarily responsible for the deterioration of the Malay society. The persistence of these views long after the advent of colonialism is manifest in studies by Wilkinson and Winstedt, who developed the ideas of their predecessors. They distinguished two systems of Malay laws, the Adat Perpateh and the Adat Temenggong. Negative assessment of the adat found in the views of their predecessors were ascribed to the Adat Temenggong. In contrast, they acclaimed and revered the Adat Perpateh.

The authors also attempted to identify the source of the ills of Malay laws. In this respect, Islam was generally perceived as one of the main factors responsible. In fact, the comparative evaluation between the two adat was borne out of the contention that the Adat Temenggong was exposed to the influence of Islam. They further highlighted the relationship between adat law and Islam, subscribing to the view that these were irreconcilable and conflicting. Hooker and Taylor explained this as due to differences in the sources of the law, and the social and historical conditions in which they originated.

Apart from these broader issues, the authors also revealed a serious concern for specific rules of adat consonant with their administrative and economic interests. Their conception of these rules was invariably influenced by the perspectives described above. Taylor's comprehension of adat inheritance laws is a case in point. Drawing upon the opinions of his predecessors, Taylor perceived adat law on inheritance as conflicting with those of Islam. He also advocated the preservation of adat on the basis that a failure to do so would result in the collapse of the social structure.

Conceptions of Malay land tenure are yet another topic of importance in adat law studies. Key issues raised by Maxwell and Swettenham, two of its foremost proponents, pertained to the question of ownership rights to land, the nature and extent of the subjects' rights in land, and other incidents of tenure incumbent upon the subjects.

Having portrayed their essential ideas, we have sought to analyse their claims based upon certain themes. In Chapter Two we examined their conception of the nature of adat law, judgments on the traits of the law and their comparative evaluation of the adat legal systems. Several inadequacies and misconceptions, which affected a more objective understanding of the adat, were revealed. Crawford's conception and evaluation, for instance, were marred by overgeneralizations, a failure to comprehend the positive attributes of the law in relation to the society in which it operates, and a lack of objectivity in appreciating the individuality of Malay laws due to a dominant notion of the superiority of English law and legal arrangements.

Inaccurate reasoning is yet another shortcoming of their evaluation. Raffles' diagnosis that Malay laws were primarily responsible for the decline of Malay society without taking into account the effects of other non-legal but equally pertinent factors which have suppressed the prosperity and stability of the Malay states is a case in point.

The evaluative comparison between the Adat Perpateh and Adat Temenggong is wanting. Both Wilkinson and Winstedt failed to appreciate the problems involved in comparing two legal systems operating within distinct social structures. Avoiding the salient features that set them apart and the effects of these on the laws is one of the limitations of their analysis. Furthermore, negative descriptions of the Adat Temenggong are often inconsistent with related provisions found in the legal digests. They also reveal a one-sided selection of elements of the law in total disregard of equally pertinent positive traits.

Even the conception of the Adat Perpateh is erroneous. By asserting that the adat was impervious to foreign influence or that it could not be amended, Winstedt and Wilkinson revealed a static conception of the adat, one that does not evolve in response to changing conditions. Such a conception is contrary to the dynamic capacity of the adat, sanctioned theoretically and manifested in the gradual evolution of aspects of the law such as those pertaining to inheritance. Wilkinson's attempt at defining adat law is also marred by a failure to perceive a distinction between adat as law and adat as the body of social rules and customs. Allegations that such a distinction is a recent development are misleading since these are based upon inaccurate translations of the legal digests.

The perceptions of Malay adat laws may have also been influenced by the interests of the colonial power. Attempts at denigrating the image of the laws served as justification for the perpetuation of British interests. Against the backdrop of indirect rule, the comparative evaluation between the two adat has revealed an effort to select and preserve what is perceived as suitable to the interests of the colonial power. Thus, the Adat Temenggong, which Wilkinson himself conceived as being progressive, is undermined, while a particular conception of the Adat Perpateh is, by contrast, upheld.

Chapter Three explored the authors' conceptions of the relationship between adat law and Islam including the extent of the latter's influence and its effects on the adat. Here again are several drawbacks. A major shortcoming stems from a scant knowledge of Islam as well as of adat law. The perception of Raffles, Wilkinson and Winstedt that adat law and Islam are irreconcilable and conflicting has revealed their inadequate consideration of the fact that in many essential aspects, Islam accommodated, harmonised with, or remained neutral to, the precepts of adat. This dynamic capacity of Islam is supported not only by the Malay legal digests but also its doctrinal principles and evidence from Islamic legal history. Furthermore, in many instances the adat has completely assimilated Islam such that to highlight a dichotomy between these two forces is misleading.

The idea strongly implied by Wilkinson and Winstedt that the Adat Perpateh is uninfluenced by Islam is also baseless. In fact, the adat is saturated with Islamic principles. In some instances, failure to perceive this may be due to misinterpretations, conscious or otherwise, of the provisions of the adat. Attempts at identifying the source of incompatibility between Islam and adat laws also reveal an inadequate understanding of the former. Arguments that the *ahadith* are alien to Malay conditions show a failure to grasp the conceptual distinction between the culturally specific and universal content of this source of Islamic law.

Inadequate knowledge of Islam is revealed in the authors' negative appraisal of its impact on adat laws. Raffles' argument that Islam created diversification in the realm of law and thereby opened the way to tyranny and general insecurity of person and property is a case in point. This opinion illustrates inadequate knowledge of the contribution of Islam in circumscribing the powers of the ruling class and defining in no uncertain terms the rights of subjects. It also reveals a lack of awareness that Islam introduced a common system of laws into the Archipelago. Furthermore, the notion expounded by Hooker that Islam created tension in society because its revealed source was incompatible with social realities is superficial in so far as it failed to evaluate the effects of such tension, some of which may have brought about positive consequences.

Attempts at propagating the view that Islamic influence on Malay laws was superficial and limited are marred both by speculative construction of terminologies found in the digests and logical fallacies. An inadequate comprehension of Islam may also have contributed to the persistence of this idea. Hooker's failure to determine as Islamic, provisions in the legal digests merely because the words "law of God" are not explicit, serves as an example.

The conception of land tenure by Maxwell and Swettenham examined in Chapter Four are influenced by the ideological interests of the colonial power in several ways. Their view that land belonged to the sovereign, for instance, provided a justification for the British to issue land legislation in the interest of colonial capitalism. Such views also facilitated transactions in land without the claims and fetters of individual rights in land. Furthermore, contextually, this served to legitimize the denial of ownership rights to Dutch grantees in Malacca. Their conception, however, is unsupported by the legal digests, which convey that un-appropriated land belongs to no man and that ownership rests with the one who appropriates it. Where the digests mention that the ruler has possession of "dead land", this, interpreted contextually, can only be taken to mean that the ruler is the custodian of the land.

An extension of the influence of colonial ideology is revealed in Maxwell's conception of the compulsory imposition of a tithe on pain of forfeiture of land. We contend that this was a device to ensure a regular source of revenue to maintain the colonial machinery. We have also argued that the question of forfeiture of land for a failure to pay a tithe cannot be justified in the light of feudal Malay society, the Malay legal digests, as well as on the grounds utilized by Maxwell, namely, Islamic law. In fact, Maxwell's perception revealed a misrepresentation of land tax in Islam and a failure to grasp the welfare spirit of the law.

The failure to pay adequate attention to the communal dimension of ownership in land also has an important bearing on the interest of colonial capitalists. The rights of the community in determining the power of alienation affects individual ownership in two ways, namely the right of sale to outsiders, in particular foreigners, and the community's right of pre-emption. In a way, the neglect to take into ample consideration this factor facilitates transactions in land, crucial for the infrastructure of colonial capitalism.

On the issue of inheritance, Chapter Four also argued that Taylor's perspective of the problem of adat inheritance laws is inadequate in so far as it fails to take into consideration forces other than Islam, which deeply influenced the transformation of this rule of adat. His view that adat and Islamic law on inheritance are irreconcilable stems from an uncritical reliance on the perspective and perceptions of his predecessors. Generally, Taylor's portrayal reveals a static and rigid conception not only of the Islamic but also adat law. His uncritical presumption of the relationship between these two sources of Malay laws prevents him from acknowledging the dynamism of these laws in evolving innumerable legal arrangements relating to inheritance in response to specific problems and conditions. His attempts to forestall the introduction of the *faraid* on the ground that it would lead to a breakdown of the Malay matrilineal social structure further reveals his static understanding of the adat. Apart from these, Taylor's comparative evaluation of the adat and Islamic inheritance laws also suffers shortcomings due to inadequate knowledge of the principles of Islamic law. Chapter Four also argued that the perspective of conflict adopted by the colonial writers is so influential that it has continued to recur in more recent scholarship touching upon the subject, as manifested in the works of de Jong and Peletz. This adversely affects a more accurate understanding of the Malay adat laws.

In Chapter Five we have examined the recurrent assertion that Malay adat law preserved and institutionalized the privileges of the Malay ruling class. Though we do not deny these claims, our overriding concern has been to establish fallacies in thinking pertaining to the source of such laws. The writers believed that Islam was a contributory factor. Yet these laws are contrary to Islamic conceptions of kingship. Malay historical sources, such as the *Sejarah Melayu* (*Malay Annals*) were utilized in this chapter to reveal that, on the contrary, Islam introduced the rule of law and regulated the arbitrary exercise of powers of Malay rulers. These principles permeated the consciousness of Malay rulers. There is also adequate evidence to suggest that the failure to perceive this may have stemmed from the writers' inability to distinguish between the feudal and the Islamic contents of the law.

These pitfalls found in the studies have serious repercussions on the understanding of Malay adat laws. Failure to conceptualize adat in relation to the society in which it operates and to portray the adat accurately and objectively distorts the image of the adat and obstructs a fair and balanced account of the laws. Furthermore, the ways in which the writers' overall concerns were conditioned by colonial interest strongly influenced their perspectives and exposition of the laws. It affected not only their judgment but also the selection of rules of adat for study. As a result, there is a lack of research into other substantive issues of adat laws equally pertinent for a more complete understanding of Malay laws. This gives rise to lacunae and a fragmented portrayal of the adat. The lack of adequate knowledge, bias and overgeneralizations of the sources of the adat law, such as Islam, also results in innumerable errors, which cloud rather than throw light upon the nature of adat laws.

BIBLIOGRAPHY

Abdul Kahar b. Bador. *Kinship and Marriage amongst the Negri Sembilan Malays*, M.A. Thesis, University of London, 1963.

Abdul Rahman b. Hj. Mohd. *Dasar-dasar Adat Perpateh*. Kuala Lumpur: Pustaka Antara, 1964.

Abdullah b. Abdul Kadir Munshi. *Kisah Pelayaran Abdullah*. Singapore: Malaysia Publication Ltd., 1965.

——. *Hikayat Abdullah*. (trans. A.H. Hill) Singapore: Oxford University Presss, 1985.

Abdullah Yusuf Ali. *The Holy Qoran* (Text, Translation and Commentary). State of Qatar: Publications of the Presidency of Islamic Courts of Affairs, 1946.

Ahmad Ibrahim. *Islamic Law in Malaya*. Singapore: Malaysian Sociological Research Institute, 1965.

Alatas, Syed Hussein. *Democracy of Islam: A Concise Exposition with Comparative Reference to Western Political Thought*. Hague: W. van Hoeve, 1956.

——. "Reconstruction of Malaysian History", in *Revue du sud-est asiatique*. No. 3, 1962.

——. "Archaeology, History and Social Sciences in Southeast Asia", in *Federation Musuems Journal*. New Series, Vol. 9, 1964.

——. "The Islamic Conception of Religion and Social Ideal", in *The Cultural Problems of Malaysia in the Context of South East Asia*. Alisjahbana, S.T., Nayagan, X.S.T., and Wang Gangwu (eds.), Kuala Lumpur: Malaysia Society of Orientalists, 1965.

——. *Thomas Stamford Raffles (1781–1826): Schemer or Reformer?* Singapore: Angus and Robertson, 1971.

——. *Modernization and Social Change*. Sydney: Angus and Roberston, 1972.

——. *The Myth of The Lazy Native*. London: Frank Cass, 1977.

——. *Kita dengan Islam*. Singapore: Pustaka Nasional, 1979.

Al-Attas, Syed Muhammad Al-Naguib. *Preliminary Statement on a General Theory of the Islamization of the Malay-Indonesian Archipelago*. Kuala Lumpur: Dewan Bahasa dan Pustaka, 1969.

——. *Islam dalam Sejarah dan Kebudayan Melayu*. Kuala Lumpur: Universiti Kebangsaan Malaysia, 1972.

Al-Ghazali. *Counsel for Kings*. (trans., by F.R.C. Bagley), London: Oxford University Press, 1961.

Allan, C.K. *Law in the Making*. Oxford: Oxford University Press, 1964.

Allport, Gordon W. *The Nature of Prejudice*. Massachusetts: Addison-Wesley, 1966.

Ameer Ali, Syed. *A Short History of the Saracens*. London: Macmillan and Company, 1899.

——. *Mohammedan Law*. 2 Vols., Calcutta: Thacker, Spink and Company, (1912–1917).

——. *The Spirit of Islam: A History of the Evolution and Ideals of Islam*. London: Christophers, 1946.

Arnold, T.W. *The Preaching of Islam*. Lahore: Ashraf, 1968.

Arnold, Thomas and Alfred Guillame (eds.), *Legacy of Islam*. Oxford: Oxford University Press, 1931.

Austin, J. *The Province of Jurisprudence Determined and the Uses of the Study of Jurisprudence*. London: Weidenfield and Nicolson, 1954.

Azhar Ibrahim Alwee. "Orientalisme Dalam Pengajaran Melayu", in *The International Conference on Malay Language, Literatured Culture II* organized by Asian Languages and Cultures, National Institute of Education, Singapore, 1–3 September, 2002.

Baillie, N.B.E. *Land Tax of India: According to the Moohamuden Law.* London: Smith Elder, 1953.

Barbossa Duarte. *The Book of Duarte Barbossa.* (trans., ed., M.L. Dames), London: Hakluyt Society, Vol. 2, 2nd Series, No. 49, 1921.

Benda, H.J. *The Crescent and the Rising Sun.* The Hague: Van Hoeve, 1958.

Blackstone, W. *Commentaries on the Laws of England.* London: Claredon Press, 1966.

Blagden, C.O. "Report of Governor Balthasar Bort on Malacca 1678", in *Journal of the Malayan Branch, Royal Asiatic Society.* Vol. V, August, 1927.

——. "Minangkabau Custom-Malacca", in *Journal of the Malayan Branch, Royal Asiatic Society.* Vol. 8, Part II, 1930.

Bloch, Marc. *Feudal Society.* London: Routledge and Kegan Paul, 1978.

Bradell, T. "Gambling and Opium Smoking in the Straits of Malacca", in *Journal of Indian Archipelago,* New Series, Vol. 1, 1856.

——. "Ancient Trade of the Indian Archipelago", in *Journal of the Indian Archipelago.* New Series, Vol. II, No. 4, 1858.

——. "The Europeans in the Indian Archipelago in the 16th and 17th Centuries", in *Journal of the Indian Archipelago.* New Series, Vol. II, No. 4, 1858.

Bukhari Al-Jauhari and Khalid Hussain (eds.), *Tajus Salatin.* Kuala Lumpur: Dewan Bahasa dan Pustaka, 1966.

Buss-Tjen, P.P. "Malay Law", in *American Journal of Comparative Law.* Vol. 7, 1958.

Caldecott, A. "Jelebu Customary Songs and Sayings", in *Journal of the Straits Branch, Royal Asiatic Society.* No. 78, June, 1918.

Cardozo, B.N. *Paradoxes of Legal Science.* Westport, Connecticut: Greenwood Press, 1928.

Carter, J.C. *Law: Its Origin, Growth and Function.* New York: G.P. Putnam, 1907.

Cherry, Richard R. *Lectures on the Growth of Criminal Law in Ancient Communities.* London: Macmillan, 1890.

Chulan, Raja. *Misa Melayu.* Kuala Lumpur: Penerbitan Pustaka Antara, 1966.

Clifford, Hugh. *A Lesson from the Malay States.* New York: Atlantic, November 1899.

Cohn, Bernard S. *Colonialism and its Forms of Knowledge.* Princeton: Princeton University Press, 1996.

Crawford, J. *History of the Indian Archipelago.* 3 Vols., Edinburgh: Archibald Constable, 1820.

Daniel, Norman. *Islam and the West: The Making of an Image.* Edinburgh: The University Press, 1960.

De Coulanges, Numa Denis Fustel. ANCIENT *City: A Study on Religion, Laws and Institutions of Greece and Rome.* New York: Doublebay and Company, 1956.

Durkheim, Emile. *The Division of Labour in Society.* (trans. by George Simpson), New York: Free Press, 1933.

Elias, Taslim Olawale. *Nature of African Customary Law.* Manchester: Manchester University Press, 1956.

Emerson, Rupert. *Malaysia: A Study in Direct and Indirect Rule.* KL: University of Malaya Press, 1964.

Erlich, Eugene. *Fundamental Principles of the Sociology of Law.* Cambridge, Massachusetts: Harvard University Press, 1936.

Evans-Pritchard, E.E. *Essays in Social Anthropology.* London: Faber and Faber, 1962.

Fanon, Frantz. *The Wretched of the Earth.* (trans., C. Farrington), London: MacGibbon and Keer, 1956.

Fatimi, S.Q. *Islam Comes to Malaysia* (ed. Shirle Gordon). Singapore: Malaysian Research Institute, 1963.

Federated Malay States. *The Land Laws and Land Administration of the Federated Malay States.* Kuala Lumpur: FMS Government Press, (1907?).

GA De C. De Moubray. *Matriarchy in the Malay Peninsula and Neighbouring Countries.* London: George Routledge, 1931.

Gluckman, Max. *Politics, Law and Ritual in Tribal Society*. Oxford: Basil Blackwell, 1965.
——. (ed.), *Ideas and Procedure in African Customary*. London: Oxford University Press, 1969.
Goitein, S.D. *Studies in Islamic History and Institutions*. Leiden: E.J. Brill, 1966.
Goldziher, Ignaz. "The Principles of Law in Islam", in *The Historian's History of the World*. New York, Vol. VIII, 1907.
——. *Muslim Studies*. 2 Vols., London: Allen and Unwin, (1967–1971).
——. *Introduction to Islamic Theology and Law*. Princeton: Princeton University Press, 1981.
Gray, J.C. *Nature and Sources of Law*. New York: Macmillan Company, 1921.
Gritner, C.A. *Book IV of the Bustan Us-Salatin* by Nurruddin Ar-Raniri. Ph.D. Thesis, School of Oriental, and African Studies, 1975.
Gullick, J.M. *Indigenous Political System of Western Malaya*. London: Athlone Press, 1965.
——. "The Negri Sembilan Economy of the 1890s", in *Journal of Malayan Branch, Royal Asiatic Society*, Vol. 24, No. 1, 1951, pp. 38–55.
Gurvitch, G. *Sociology of Law*. London: Routledge and Kegan Paul, 1947.
Gibb, H.A.R. and J.H. Kramars (eds.), *Shorter Encyclopedia of Islam*. Leiden: E.J. Brill, 1953.
Hart, H.L.A *Concept of Law*. Oxford: Clarendon Press, 1961.
Hill, A.H. (trans.) "Hikayat Raja-Raja Pasai", in *Journal of the Malayan Branch, Royal Asiatic Society*. Vol. 33, Part 2, 1960.
Hobson, J.S. *Imperialism*. London: Allen and Unwin, 1938.
Hoebel, E. Adamson. *The Law of Primitive Man*. Cambridge, Mass.: Harvard University Press, 1954.
Holmes, Oliver Wendel. *Collected Legal Papers*. New York: Harcourt Brace, 1923.
Hooker, Michael Barry. "Interaction of Legislation and Customary Law in a Malay State", *American Journal of Comparative Law*. Vol. 16, 1968.
——. "A Note on the Malay Legal Digests", in *Journal of the Malayan Branch, Royal Asiatic Society*. Vol. 41, Part I, July, 1968.
——. (ed.), *Readings in Malay Adat Laws*. Singapore: Singapore University Press, 1970.
——. "Law, Religion and Bureaucracy in a Malay State: A Study in Conflicting Power Centers", in *American Journal of Comparative Law* Vol. 19, 1971.
——. *Adat Laws in Modern Malaya*. Kuala Lumpur: Oxford University Press, 1971.
——. "Challenge of Malay Adat Law in the Realm of Comparative Law", in *International and Comparative Law Quarterly*. Vol. 22, 1973.
——. "Introduction: Islamic Law in South-east Asia", in *Studia Islamika*, Vol. 10, No. 1, 2003.
——. "The Trengganu Inscription in Malayan Legal History", in *Journal of the Malayan Branch, Royal Asiatic Society*. Vol. 49, Part II, 1976.
Huizinga, Johan. *The Waning of the Middle Ages*. Middlesex: Penguin Books, 1972.
Ibn Khaldun. *The Muqaddimah: An Introduction to the Study of History*. (trans., F. Rosenthal), London: Routledge and Kegan Paul, 1976.
Ismail bin Mat. *Adat and Islam in Malaysia: A Study in Legal Conflict and Resolution*. Thesis (PhD), Temple University, 1985.
Jafri Asbari (trans.) *Nahjul Balagha: Sermons, Letters and Sayings of Imam Ali Ibn Abi Talib*. Accra: Islamic Seminary Publications, 1984.
Jong, Josselin de. "Islam versus Adat in Negri Sembilan (Malaya)", in *Bijdragen tot de Taal-Land en Volkenkunde*, 116, 1960.
——. *Minangkabau and Negri Sembilan: Socio-Political Structure in Indonesia*. Bhratara, Djakarta, 1960.
Joseph, K.T. "Malacca Land Laws", in *Federation Museums Journal*. Vol. XV, 1970.
Kempe, John E. and R.O. Winstedt (eds.), "A Malay Legal Digest Compiled for 'Abd al-Ghafur Muhauiyu'd-din Shah Sultan of Pahang 1592–1614 AD", in *Journal of the Malayan Branch, Royal Asiatic Society*. Vol. XXI, Part I, 1948.

Kern, Fritz. *Kingship and Law in the Middle Ages*. Oxford: B. Blackwell, 1948.
Kernial Singn Sandhu, Paul Wheatley (eds.), *Melaka: The Transformation of a Malay Capital c. 1400–1980*. Kuala Lumpur: Oxford University Press, 1983.
Khadduri Majid (ed.), *Law in the Middle East*. Washington: Middle East Institute, 1995.
Khadduri Majid (trans.), *Islamic Jurisprudence: Shafi'i's Risala*. Baltimore: John Hopkins Press, 1961.
Khadduri Majid. *The Islamic Conception of Justice*. Baltimore: John Hopkins University Press, 1984.
Kuczynski, J. *Great Britain 1750 to the Present Day*. Vol. 1, Part I. A Short History of Labour Conditions Under Industrial Capitalism. London: Fredrick. Muller, 1942.
Kuppaswami Alladi. *Mayne's Hindu law and Usage*. New Delhi: Bharat House, 1986.
Lev, Daniel S. *Islamic Courts in Indonesia: A Study in the Political Bases of Legal Institutions*. Berkeley: University of California Press, 1972.
Lim Teck-Ghee. *Origins of a Colonial Economy: Land and Agriculture in Perak, 1874–1897*. Penang: Penerbit University Sains Malaysia, 1976.
Linton, Ralph. *The Study Of Man*. New York: Appleton-Century-Crofts, 1964.
Llewellyn, K.N. and Adamson E. Hoebel. *The Cheyenne Way: Conflict and Case Law in Primitive Justice*. Norman: University of Oklahoma Press, 1941.
Logan, J.R. "On the Laws of the Indian Archipelago and Eastern Asia", in *Journal of the Indian Archipelago*. Vol. 1, 1847.
Macfie, A.L. (ed.), *Orientalism: A Reader*. New York: New York University Press, 2000.
MacIver Robert. *Society*. London: Macmillan Press, 1937.
——. *The Web of Government*. New York: Macmillan, 1965.
Majul, Cesar Adib. "Theories on the Spread of Islam in Malaysia", in *Siliman Journal*. Vol. XI, No. 4, October–December, 1964, Philippines: Dumaguete City.
Malinowski, Bronislow. *Coral Gradens and Their Magic: A Study of Methods of Filling the Soil and of Agricultural Rites in the Trobriand Islands*. London: George Allen and Unwin, 1935.
——. *Crime and Custom in Savage Society*. London: Routledge and Kegan Paul, 1966.
Manheim, Karl. *Ideology and Utopia* (trans. by Louis Wirth and Edward Shils), New York: Harcourt, Brace and Company, 1936.
——. *Essays on Sociology and Social Psychology*. London: Routledge and Kegan Paul, 1953.
Marsden, William. *History of Sumatra*. London: Oxford University Press, 1966.
Marx, Karl and Frederick Engels. *On Colonialism*. Moscow: Progress Publishers, 1968.
Maunier, Rene. *Sociology of Colonies*. (ed. and trans. E.O. Lorimer), London: Routledge and Kegan Paul, 1949.
Maxwell, W.E. "Law and Customs of Malays with Reference to Tenure of Land", in *Journal of the Straits Branch, Royal Asiatic Society*. No. 13, June, 1884.
——. "The Law Relating to Slavery among the Malays", in *Journal of the Straits Branch, Royal Asiatic Society*. No. 22, December, 1890.
——. *Memorandum on the Introduction of a Land Code in the Native States of Malay Peninsula*, Singapore 1894.
Maznah Sharifah Syed Omar. *Myths and the Malay Ruling Class: A Study of Values and Thinking Reflected in the Hikayat*. M.A. Thesis, University of Singapore, 1985.
Meek, C.K. *Land Law and Custom in the Colonies*. London: Oxford University Press, 1946.
Mills, L.A. *British Malaya: 1824–67*. Singapore: Nanyang Printers, 1961.
Mochtar Naim (ed.), *Menggali Hukum Tanah dan Hukum Waris Minangkabau*. Padang Indonesia: Center for Minangkabau Studies Press, 1968.
Muhammad Khalid Masud. *Muslim Jurist's Quest for the Normative Basis of Shari'a*. Leiden: ISIM, 2001.

Muhammad Natsir. *Capita Selecta*. Djakarta: Bulan Bintang, 1973.
Muller, Hendrick. "The Malay Peninsula and Europe in the Past", in *Journal of the Straits Branch, Royal Asiatic Society*, Vol. LXVII, p. 79.
Muslim. Sahih Muslim. (trans. Abdul Hamid Siddiqi), Kitab Bhavan, New Delhi, (1974–1978).
Nadel, G.H. and P. Curtis (eds.), *Imperialism and Colonialism*. New York: Macmillan, 1964.
Nawawi. *Minhaj et Talibin: A Manual of the Mahammadan Law According to the School of Shafie*. London: W. Thacker, 1914
Newbold, T.J. *Political and Statistical Account of the British Settlements in the Straits of Malacca*. 2 Vols., London: John Murray, 1839.
Nietzsche, Fredrich. On the Geneology of Morals. (ed., Walter Kaufman). New York: Vintage Books, 1969.
Nuru'd-din ar Randiri. *Bustanu's Salatin. Bab II, Fasal 13* (disusun oleh Iskandar, T.), Kuala Lumpur: Dewan Bahasa dan Pustaka, 1966.
Ortega Gasset. *Revolt of the Masses*. New York: The New American Library, 1950.
Othman, Ishak. *Hubungan antara Undang-Undang Islam dan Undang-Undang Adat*. Kuala Lumpur: Dewan Bahasa dan Pustaka, 1979.
Peletz, Michael Gates. *A Share of the Harvest: Kinship, Property and Social History Among the Malays of Rembau*. Berkeley: University of California Press, 1988.
——. *Social History and Evolution in the Interrelationship of Adat and Islam in Rembau, Negeri Sembilan*. Research Notes and Discussion Paper No. 27. Institute of Southeast Asian Studies, Singapore, 1981.
Pires, Tom. *The Suma Oriental of Tom Pires*. (trans., ed., Armande Cortesao), Hakluyt Society, Vol. 2, 2nd. Series, No. 90, London, 1944.
Pound, Roscoe. "The Scope and Purpose of Sociological Jurisprudence", in *Harvard Law Review*. Vol. XXV, No. 6, April, 1912.
——. *Ideal Element in Law*. University of Calcutta, 1958.
Powers, David S. "The Maliki Family Endowment: Legal Norms and Social Practices", in *International Journal of Middle East Studies*, Vol. 25, No. 3 (Aug., 1993), 379–406.
Radcliffe-Brown, A.R. *Structure and Function of Primitive Society*. London: Cohen and West, 1952.
Raffles, Thomas Stamford. *Memoirs*. 2 Vols., (ed. Sophia Raffles), London: James Duncan, 1835.
Rahman Rahim. *Nilai-Nilai Utama Kebudayaan Bugis*. Lembaga Penerbitan Universitas Hasanuddin, 1985.
Riau, Raja Ali al-Haji. *Tuhfat al-Nafis*. Singapore: Malaysia Publications, 1965.
Roff, William R. *The Origins Of Malay Nationalism*. Kuala Lumpur: University of Malaya Press, 1967.
Rushe, G. and Otto Kircheimer. *Punishment and Social Structure*. New York: Russel and Russel, 1939.
Ruskin, John. *Unto this Last*. Kent: George Allen, 1888.
Sadler, G.T. *Relation of Custom to Law*. London: Sweet and Maxwell, 1919.
Said, Edward W. *Orientalism*. London: Routledge and Kegan Paul, 1978.
Schact, Josheph. *Origins of Muhammadan Jurisprudence*. Oxford: Clarendon Press, 1950.
——. *Introduction to Islamic Law*. Clarendon Press, Oxford, 1964.
Schrieke, B. *Effects of Western Influence on Native Civilizations in the Malay Archipelago*. Batavia: Kolff, 1929.
——. *Indonesian Sociological Studies*. W. van Hoeve, The Hague, 1957.
Shaharuddin Maaruf. *Concept of a Hero in Malay Society*. Singapore: Eastern Universities Press, 1984.
Sharif, M.M. (ed.), *A History of Muslim Philosophy*. 2 Vols., Wiesbaden: Otto Harrassowitz, 1963.
Shellabear, W.G. (ed.), *Sejarah Melayu*. Kuala Lumpur: Oxford University Press, 1967.

——. *Malay Ideas on Development: From Feudal Lord to Capitalist.* Singapore: Times Books International, 1988.

Siti Hawa Salleh (ed.) *Hikayat Merong Mahawangsa.* Kuala Lumpur: University of Malaya Press, 1970.

Snouck Hurgronje, C. *The Achehnese.* 2 Vols., (trans., A.W.S. O'Sullivan), Leiden, 1906.

Sorokin, Pitirim. Social and Cultural Dynamics. Vol. 2. *Fluctuations of Systems of Truth, Ethics and Law.* New York: American Book Co., (1937–1941).

——. *Power and Morality.* Massachusettes: Porter Sargent, 1959.

Suminto, H. Aqib. *Islam di Indonesia: Politik Hindia Belanda.* Singapore: Pustaka Nasional, 1985.

Swettenham, F.A. *British Malaya.* London: Allen and Unwin, 1955.

Syarifuddin, Amir. *Pelaksanaan Hukum Kewarisan Islam Dalam Lingkungan Adat Minanagkabau.* Jakarta: Gunung Agung, 1984.

Taufik Abdullah. "Adat and Islam: An Examination of Conflict in Minangkabau", *Indonesia*, 1966, vol. 2, pp. 1–24.

Tawney, R.H. *Agrarian Problems of the Sixteenth Century.* New York: Longmans Green, 1912.

——. *The Acquisitive Society.* New York: Harcourt, Brace and Weld, 1920.

——. *Religion and the Rise of Capitalism.* London: John Murray, 1960.

Taylor, E.N. "Malay Family Law", in *Journal of Malayan Branch, Royal Asiatic Society*, Vol VX, Pt. 1, 1937.

Ter Haar, B. *Adat Law in Indonesia* (eds., Hoebel, E. Adamson; Schiller, A. Arthur). New York: Institute of Pacific Relations, 1948.

Tham Seong Chee. *Malays and Moderniszation: A Sociological Interpretation.* Singapore: Singapore University press, 1977.

——. "Tradition, Values and Society among the Malays", in *Review of S.E. Asian Studies.* Vol. 1, No. 4, Dec. 1971.

Van Vollenhoven. *Van Vollenhoven on Indonesian Adat Law.* (ed. J.H. Holleman), Martinus Nijhoff, The Hague, 1981.

Vinagradoff, P. *Custom and Right.* Oslo: Ascheoug and Company, 1925.

Voon Phin Keong. *Indebtedness and Land Use in Pre-War Malaya.* KL.: University of Malaya, 1987

Wade, E.C.S. and A.W. Bradley. *Constitutional Law.* London: Longmans, 1965.

Watt, W.M. *Muhammed at Mecca.* Oxford: Clarendon Press, 1953.

Weber, Max. *On Law in Economy and Society.* (ed. Reinstein, Max) Cambridge: Harvard University Press, 1925.

Wertheim, W.F. *East-West Parallels.* Van Hoeve, The Hague, 1964.

——. *Indonesian Society in Transition.* The Hague: Van Hoeve, 1964.

Wilkinson, R.J. "Mohammedan Law in Malaya", in *Papers on Malay Subjects.* Vol. 2, Pt. 1, FMS. Kuala Lumpur: Government Press, 1908.

Winstedt, R.O. "An Old Minangkabau Legal Digest from Perak", in *Journal of the Malayan Branch, Royal Asiatic Society.* Vol. XXVI, Part 1, July 1953.

——. *The Malays: A Cultural History.* Singapore: Kelly and Walsh, 1956.

Winstedt, R.O. (ed.), "Kedah Laws", in *Journal of the Malayan Branch, Royal Asiatic Society.* Vol. 6, June, 1928.

Winstedt, R.O. and Josselin de Jong (eds.), "A Digest of Customary Law from Sungei Ujong", in *Journal of the Malayan Branch*, Royal Asiatic Society. Vol. XXVII, Part 3, July, 1954.

——. *Malaya and Its History.* London: Hutchinson, 1953.

Wong, David S.Y. *Tenure and Land Dealings in the Malay States.* Singapore: Singapore University Press, 1975.

Yeger, Moshe. *Islam and Islamic Institutions in British Malaya: Policies and Implementation.* Jerusalem: The Magnes Press, 1979.

INDEX

SOCIAL SCIENCES IN ASIA

1. Thang, L. L. and W.-H. Yu (eds.). *Old Challenges, New Strategies*. Women, Work and Family in Contemporary Asia. 2004. ISBN 90 04 13732 7
2. Lyons, L. *State of Ambivalence*. The Feminist Movement in Singapore. 2005. ISBN 90 04 13139 6
3. Hassan, R. (ed.). *Local and Global: Social Transformation in Southeast Asia*. Essays in Honour of Professor Syed Hussein Alatas. 2005. ISBN 90 04 14158 8
4. Ho, E. P. *Times of Change*. A Memoir of Hong Kong's Governance 1950-1991. 2005. ISBN 90 04 14047 6
5. Baber, Z. (ed.). *CyberAsia*. The Internet and Society in Asia. 2006. ISBN 90 04 14625 3
6. Abdul Rahman, N. A. *Colonial Image of Malay Adat Laws*. A Critical Appraisal of Studies on Adat Laws in the Malay Peninsula during the Colonial Era and Some Continuities. 2006. ISBN 90 04 15056 0
7. Lian, K. F. (ed.). *Race, Ethnicity, and the State in Malaysia and Singapore*. 2006. ISBN 90 04 15096 X

ISSN 1567-2794